The Bad Girl's Guide to the Party Life

The Bad Girl's

Illustrations by Susannah Bettag

Guide to the Party Life

by Cameron Tuttle

CHRONICLE BOOKS
SAN FRANCISCO

Bad Girl's Guide™ and Bad Girl Swirl™ are trademarks
of Bad Girl Swirl, Inc.

Library of Congress Cataloging-in-Publication Data available.

ISBN 0-8118-3361-5

Printed in the United States of America.

Designed by Pamela Geismar

Distributed in Canada by Raincoast Books
9050 Shaughnessy Street
Vancouver, British Columbia V6P 6E5

10 9 8 7 6 5 4 3 2 1

Chronicle Books LLC
85 Second Street
San Francisco, California 94105

www.chroniclebooks.com

You know it's time to throw a party when you stop hanging up on telemarketers.

Contents

HELLO MY NAME IS

Ms. Baddy Manners

Contents

Directions to the party life:

Date: _____

Party Prescriptions

Signed: _____ *Dr. Bad Girl* _____

RSVP CARD

M_____ *would like to*

You are invited to. . .

Contents

Thank You Note

The Order of Events

If you want to read the book in order:

Acknowledgments

Who knew that a little pink book about road tripping could start all this? Wow. Full-body thanks to all the bad girls around the world who are spreading the Bad Girl gospel and keeping my dream alive. This book's for you!

To everyone on Team Bad Girl, my personal and professional pit crew, I'm grateful for your enthusiasm, ideas, inspiration, and support, especially Julie Mason, Leslie Kirby, A.M. Drury, Kimberly Wiefling, Raymond Long, Linda Jones, Amy Robinson, Charlotte Sheedy, and Susannah Bettag, whose brilliant illustrations bring my simple words to life.

As always, many thanks to the talented individuals at Chronicle Books with whom I am very fortunate to work: Pamela Geismar, Jay Schaefer, Steve Mockus, Brenda Tucker, Kerry Colburn, and free agent Kate Chynoweth.

To the wild cards with wild ideas I lovingly appropriated for the cause: Joanne Papini, Stephanie Williams, Susannah Bruder, Danielle Beverly, Deborah Bishop, Tracy Coombe, and Becky Masline, who graciously taught me everything I know about the knee fart.

Warm, wet thanks to the baddies of badgirlswirl.com. You never stop amazing me with your smarts and baditude. You're the real deal, the original bad girls who get it. I wish I could list each one of you but I only get a page: Gax, MissAloo, zeelee, Metroprincess, Volvita, LittleSprout, Nikakat79, FreakyFruit Barracuda, Wickedfairy, Macaroon_Vespa, CandyCane_Jaguar, PrincessLindsay, Gypsyspice, phx bad girl, moonburn, Devildoll, Barracuda, tangogrrrl, punk style, Heathergirl, Paella_Diablo, linzee, MsCommunication, DarkPhoenix8, Melhuss, leighchristine, Steppenwolf_Babe, woobee, Kheperan_Phoenix, Caviar_Ferrari, Talulabelle, edible_karamel_condoms, ophelias_revenge, Yaz, * kitten *, and TrixiePixie.

Let's party!

The Party Life

*Y*ou can play now or you can play later. But why wait to celebrate? Good girls believe in the afterlife, bad girls believe in the Party Life—that divine state of being devoted to celebrating fun, your friends, yourself, and the life you have here and now. No matter who you are or how you like to celebrate, the Party Life is where you shine.

Every enlightened bad girl glitters in the Party Life, sparkling with confidence as everything comes together in perfect social order. You know the feeling. You're hanging with friends. You're feeling relaxed, smart, funny, and a little full of yourself. You're in the moment and in your groove, wearing something bad and saying something badder. Then, when life couldn't possibly get any better, your favorite song comes on. Suddenly, you're filled with the Party Life force! You start shakin' your booty. You feel the love around you. You see your bad girl aura shining bright above the crowd. You've found bliss in the party life—your party nirvana. Imagine feeling that vibe all the time.

Living the Party Life is not just about going to parties. It's about celebrating yourself, your life, and everything around you—even some of the less-than-perfect things. When you step into the Party Life, the harsh lights dim, your mood brightens, and your perspective changes. Suddenly, you hear the music in the honking horns, you see the confetti in the chaos, you feel the pleasure in the

11

pain. You realize that you are the bad-girl belle of your ball, the shooting star of your show, and the party mojo mistress. It's your life—you get to make the guest list, name the theme, and select your costume.

When you're living the Party Life, you're living the feel-good life, choosing to celebrate whatever makes you feel good. Celebrate your hair, your butt, your laugh, your eyes. Celebrate your imagination, your smile, your shoes, your thighs. Celebrate your past, your present, and your future mistakes. Celebrate your weirdest behavior and your strangest fantasies. Celebrate your personal power to choose—your friends, your job, your food, your mood, your fun. Celebrate your freedom to be the bad girl of your wildest dreams.

Your Party Mantra

Before you can experience the party life, you must be clear on your spiritual party path. Start by envisioning your personal party nirvana, then select a mantra to guide you there. Before you leave for any party, breathe deeply and repeat your mantra three times. If you begin to feel yourself wandering off course during the evening, simply retreat to a quiet bathroom, bedroom, or closet and repeat your mantra until you rediscover your strength and your way. (Of course, your mantra will also center you at home, at the office, or wherever you are when craving the party life.)

from the bathroom wall into your Palm Pilot. You know it's time to leave a party

Party Life Plan	Personal Mantra
Feel confident and in control	"I'm smart enough, I'm bad enough, and gosh darn it, people like me!"
Celebrate big-butt beauty	"Bottoms up, girls!"
Stay positive, no matter what	"When the party life hands me lemons, I make a stiff lemon drop."
Let go and join in on the fun	"Left hand, green!"
Experience personal power	"Take a number, boys."
Get great action in bed	"I gave at the office. I'm here to get."
Get naked with an evil ex	"Love the sin, hate the sinner."
Get naked with a born-again bad boy	"Hate the sin, love the sinner!"
Get respect	"No means no, you ho!"
Be open to new experiences	"Yes please!"
Be open to new people	"Pretty please, with a cherry on top!"
Accept the party life	"Let go and let bad."
Avoid long bathroom lines	"When nature calls, I go to it!"
Spread love, joy, and the bad girl gospel	"Spin the Bottle or Truth or Bare?"

when the host is getting ready for work. You know it's time to throw a party when

the power of the party life

If you want to feel the power of the Party Life, you've got to believe in it—every day in every way. When you think positive party thoughts 24-7, you'll have more fun than a bad girl on a get-down-and-boogie bender. And who doesn't want that?

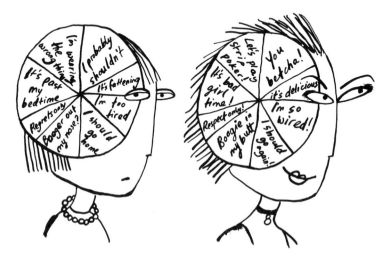

Party Pooper
I'm too tired.
I probably shouldn't.
It's past my bedtime.
Booger out my nose?
I'm wearing the wrong thing.
It's fattening.
I should go home.
Regrets only.

Party Lifer
I'm so wired!
You betcha!
It's bad girl time!
Boogie in my butt!
Let's play strip poker!
It's delicious!
I should go again!
Respect only!

your last three social outings were weddings or baby showers. You know it's time

Join the Bad Girl Party!

Being bad isn't just a personality type, it's an underground political movement. Bad girls everywhere are joining forces to fuel their collective power and make the world a badder place, one girl at a time. If you think this party is tied to a bunch of special interest groups, you're right! The Bad Girl Party is interested in special groups having fun, celebrating every day, and laughing at the absurdity and joys of life.

To form your own local chapter of the Bad Girl Party, just gather your personal posse together, don raspberry berets, pink bandanas, inflated condoms, or other empowering headwear, place one hand on your hip, and shout the "we believes." (Feel free to add your own to reflect personal preferences, regional taste, and local color.)

We are the Bad Girl Party . . .

We believe in the power of one and the power of fun.

We believe in independent thinking.

We believe in the pleasure principle.

We believe in speaking our minds.

We believe in challenging the status quo.

We believe in shoes.

We believe in celebrating anything and everything.

We believe in freedom of choice when shopping, dating, and mating.

We believe in the right to bare arms, shoulders, and our bad girl souls.

We believe in living the dream.

We believe in ourselves.

We believe it's time to party!

to leave a party when you're the funniest person there. You know it's time to throw

A Typical Girl's Party Transformation

When you're a bad girl, you're the life of every party!

House Party	6:00 p.m.	9:00 p.m.	Midnight
How you say hello:	Friendly handshake	Friendly butt squeeze	Friendly French kiss
Appearance:	Hair perfectly done Light makeup, tastefully applied Age-appropriate party dress	Hair artfully undone A bit sweaty and sexy Partly undressed	Giving free hair-styling tips to all guests Too dark to tell but sure tastes great Modeling the hostess's tennis dress
Worries:	Was I invited out of pity or by mistake? Will anyone want to talk to me? Can you see my slip?	Who invited her? Will anyone want to dance with me? Will I make another raunchy Freudian slip?	Who can I still call to invite? Will everyone want to talk to me, dance with me, and compete to take me home again tonight? Will anyone take me up on my next raunchy Freudian slip?
Attitude:	I don't have time to party—I've got too much work to do.	I don't have time not to party! This should be my full-time job!	I love you guys! Let's all quit our jobs and start a business so we can be together every day! I'll be the CEO, what can you do?
Conversation topics:	Cruelty-free testing Serious politics Foreign films 401(k) strategies	Cruelty-free kissing Steamy office politics Sexual fantasies I'm okay, you're okay strategies	Cruelty-free living Who you'd do on *West Wing* Sexual fantasies with foreigners Getting to BK strategies

	Republican or Democrat?	Filtered or unfiltered?	Astroglide or KY?
Whispered question:			
Party to-do list:	Write down host's address so you can send timely thank-you note. Touch up lipstick every 20 minutes. Panic over wine stain on party dress.	Write no-thank-you note on panty-liner and slap on rude dude's chest. Touch cute guest every 20 minutes. Dirty dance until wine-stained party dress is drenched in sweat.	Write juicy party details on upper thigh for hilarious, tell-all memoir. Touch self every 20 minutes. Hang dress over shower bar to dry and return to the dirty dance floor.
Best dance move:	The nervous toe tap	The bump and grind	The diving catch to save a crystal vase filled with Ketel One and cranberry
Sex life:	Yeah, whatever. Sex is overrated.	Yeah, baby. Just thinking about it gets me overheated.	Yeah, I'm talking to you. Get over here.
Religious outlook:	Lord help me.	God bless this drink!	With God as my witness, I must have been a Solid Gold Dancer in a former life!
Transportation plans:	I'm the designated driver and plan to drive myself home.	I'm the designated partier and plan to take a cab home.	I'm the designated Bad Girl and have no plans to go home.
Party highlights:	Nothing stuck in teeth Met some interesting new people Didn't get drunk, nervous, hyper, or make a fool of myself	Mule stuck to kitchen floor Met my new best friend Didn't light the wrong end of a cigarette	Stuck to sexy shirtless dancing machine Drove to Vegas and got married! Shaved my head in the host's bathroom (made $200!)

Extend Your Party Life Span

With the right attitude and a little event planning, you can bring the Party Life to life anywhere.

At the office

* Decorate your cubicle with big balloons and bright-colored streamers.
* At your next business meeting, give out party hats and favors in addition to the agenda. When the work is done, suggest a friendly game of musical chairs.
* In a crowded elevator, be outgoing and introduce yourself to the other guests. Before you get off the elevator, be sure to say something friendly like, "I'm going to the bar, can I get you anything?"

At home

* Hang a disco ball from the kitchen ceiling, direct a few flashlights at it, then turn down the lights, turn up the volume on your favorite disco CD, and expose your roommate, pet, or spying neighbor to a little Saturday Night Fever.
* Pass yummy Pounce treats to the neighborhood cats on a silver tray. You'll be the most popular girl at your block party in no time!
* After brushing your teeth, stare at yourself in the mirror, smile flirtatiously, and ask, "Have we met?" Then give yourself a couple of Euro air kisses good night.

a party when your cousin's bar mitzvah sounds like fun. You know it's time to

In the car

* Transform your car into a rolling disco ball by spraying it with hairspray and dusting it with silver glitter.
* Crank your best dance mix, put the pedal to the metal, and car dance until you're sweaty and exhausted or pulled over by a cop.
* When stuck in traffic, pass hors d'oeuvres to nearby motorists, make friendly small talk, and suggest fun ice-breaker party games . . . "Hey, want to play Truth or Dare?"

At the gym

* Work out in a fabulous evening gown with a feather boa.
* Wear a pantyliner nametag that says, "Hello, my name is _____." When members arrive to work out, say, "Thanks for coming! Love your outfit! Can I take your coat?"
* Casually work the crowd, getting to know everyone in the weight room. Don't forget to introduce the cute single guys to the cute single girls!

19

leave a party when you're playing Spin the Bottle with yourself. You know it's time

Past Life Converter

Every girl is entitled to a Party Life. No matter how pathetic your past life has been, you're in. All you need is a little attitude adjustment. Remember: Good things come to those who celebrate!

Past Life	Party Life
Can't get a date?	Celebrate your independence!
Can't find a job?	Celebrate your freedom!
Can't get a cab?	Celebrate your shoes and dance in the street!
Can't get any action?	Celebrate your vibrator!
Can't get anyone to take you seriously?	Celebrate your sense of humor!
Can't shake an old reputation?	Celebrate your sense of rumor!
Can't sing on key?	Celebrate your rhythm section!
Can't fill your bra?	Celebrate and take it off!
Can't balance your checkbook?	Celebrate your creativity!
Can't lose weight?	Celebrate your big ole butt!

the bad girl's porta-party

Today's most fashionable party lifer is pret-a-parté—bad girl speak for ready to rock. She's got the right attitude, music, and accessories to turn the dullest activity into a raucous celebration in the wink-wink of an eye. With Porta-Party hostess skills, waiting in line at the car wash, post office, DMV, or gynecologist's office isn't a waste of time—it's party time! Use these tips to start the Porta-Party that's right for your situation and personal style.

Beach Blanket Bad Girl

Think Annette Funicello and her perky friends on the Ecstasy Channel.

porta-party carrier: guitar case

essentials: polka dot bikinis, wind-blown attitude, big blanket, Frisbee, hors d'oeuvre tray, beach ball, box of fine wine, plastic cups (can double as bikini tops in a pinch—just wet, press, and let suction do the rest)

extras: glow-in-the-dark astronomy guide, boom box with beach tunes, sparklers for midnight games of spot the big skinny dipper

best venues: car wash and mall with a fountain

Jane Bond Bad Girl

Think the secret love child of James Bond and Jane Fonda (pre-Ted) on a three-flirtini-lunch.

porta-party carrier: a black attaché

essentials: sexy, self-confident attitude, witty banter, cock-tail shaker and booty-shakin' tunes, silver flask of vodka, plus vermouth and olives (for martinis), chilled Kiwi and

21

Strawberry Snapple (for quickie Cosmos), chilled Peach Snapple (for tasty Sex on the Beach cocktails)

extras: olives (to toss at passing motorists and pedestrians), lemon wedges for freshening cocktails and breath before politically incorrect mouth-to-mouth resuscitation of dangerous foreigner

best venues: swank hotel lobby and high-rise rooftop (with plenty of voyeurs in view)

Solid Gold Bad Girl

Think your braces-wearing self dancing in front of the TV—with (finally!) sexy grown-up moves and grooves.

porta-party carrier: purple suede fringe shoulder bag

Party Prescriptions from

Dr. Bad Girl

....

Your symptoms:
You did something naughty, didn't get caught, and feel very guilty

Your bad girl cure:
Throw a Bad Girl Confessional Party!
• Set up a not-at-all-confidential confessional.
• All bad girls must confess their baddest sins.
• As penance, everyone must drink three Bloody
  Marys and confess how they'd do four of our fathers.

---

know it's time to leave a party when you're spooning with the host's cat. You know

essentials: '70s attitude—and hair, dance-mix CD (e.g., soundtrack to *Saturday Night Fever,* Donna Summer, etc.) and boom box, this book and a flashlight

extras: platform shoes, skin-tight bell bottoms, off-the-shoulder halter top, body glitter and hair spray, dance moves to the Hustle

best venues: crowded subway platform and laundromat

La Vida Bad Girl

Think the secret love child of Ricky Martin and Carmen Miranda on a nightclub stage.

porta-party carrier: large piñata

essentials: a hot Latin attitude, tight low-cut pants, tequila in an off-the-shoulder *cantina,* chilled Fresca for margarita mix, crushed ice to cool off the crowd

extras: salt and lime, chips and salsa served in a sombrero, great salsa music on tape or CD, vague memory of salsa steps

best venues: Catholic church and produce section of the grocery store

Super Model Bad Girl

Think the secret love child of Kate Moss and Isaac Mizrahi on the Catwalk Channel.

porta-party carrier: Kate Spade tote bag

essentials: fabulous attitude, champagne on ice pack, acrylic champagne flutes, black and

it's time to throw a party when the cigarette smoke wafting up from the street white feather boas, disposable flash cameras for paparazzi effect

extras: party poppers, celery and carrot sticks (not to be eaten under any circumstances), cigarettes (eat all you want), a pink bandana for snapping at cute guys' butts

best venues: DMV (the cameras are always clicking) and Target or Wal-Mart, where every aisle is a fabulous runway

Country Bitchin' Bad Girl

Think young, foxy Martha Stewart on a free-range bender.

porta-party carrier: a wicker picnic basket

essentials: hand-stitched picnic blanket made of butter lettuce or other organic material, spiked homemade lemonade in antique mason jars, bunch of country-fresh flowers in a vase of hand-glued sea glass, squash blossoms stuffed with Cheez Whiz

extras: airline-size booze bottles crafted into sassy dangle earrings, organic earthworm casting kit to attract passersby

best venues: Home Depot and garden center or nursery (while running errands)

Other Stylish Porta-Party Carriers

* bowling ball bag
* Powerpuff Girls knapsack
* cat carrier
* diaper bag
* tool box
* luggage on wheels
* welder's canvas utility bag
* witch's cauldron

smells good. You know it's time to leave a party when you're being escorted out in

More Great Porta-Party Venues

Realtor's open house *(Why buy the house when you can get the party milk for free?)*

Bumper-to-bumper traffic *(Road rage? No way! Road Rave? You betcha!)*

Unemployment office *(Wahoo! Another pink-slip party!)*

Any fast food restaurant *(Don't buy an action figure, be an action figure!)*

Public library *(Whisper sweet bad things in someone's ear.)*

Public transportation *(Get downtown and boogie with new friends!)*

Nail salon *(You're already high on the fumes, now crank the tunes!)*

Jury duty *(Twelve is such a nice number for parties.)*

Traffic school *(A fun way to bump into exciting people!)*

handcuffs. You know it's time to throw a party when you break out your dance

How Bad Girl Is Your

1. As a party guest, I never lift _____.
A. my fork until the hostess lifts hers
B. a finger unless asked
C. my skirt before 11:00 P.M. (unless the hostess lifts hers)

2. My favorite kooky party game is _____.
A. charades
B. limbo dancing
C. throw all the cell phones out the window

3. When trying to enter a conversation cluster, I _____.
A. wait patiently until noticed, wearing a warm smile
B. clear my throat, belt out, "Excuse me!" then clear my throat again
C. spill an ice-cold drink at crotch level

4. The naughtiest thing I've ever done at a party is _____.
A. poured a very stiff drink
B. poured a very stiff drink in a potted plant
C. peed in a potted plant

5. The party hostess should never drink so much that she _____.
A. can't remember her guests' names
B. can't remember where she put the corkscrew
C. can't remember who she just screwed

6. Whenever I host a party, I make a point to _____.
A. introduce every guest, adding a unique personal detail
B. introduce feuding ex-lovers just to watch the sparks fly
C. introduce every hottie to the hostess's VIP boudoir lounge

7. When throwing a party, the host can always count on me to _____.
A. bring a nice bottle of red wine
B. start stimulating conversations with other guests
C. stimulate other guests in the host's bedroom

8. The last time I got down and boogied like a bad girl, I _____.
A. got a little sweaty
B. got a little kinky
C. got a concussion

9. "Regrets only" at the bottom of an invitation means _____.
A. call only if you can't make the party
B. call only if you regret being invited
C. come only if you're prepared to do something you'll later regret

10. When I'm ready for the party to end but my guests won't leave, I casually _____.
A. collect used cocktail glasses and ashtrays
B. turn off all of the lights in the house and go to bed
C. call 911 and report suspicious trespassers

Party Life? [A Quiz]

11. When I notice a lull in the conversation, I usually _____.
A. bring out some fresh hors d'oeuvres
B. bring up a controversial issue for debate
C. bring up a controversial issue about my date

12. The last time people pointed and stared at me at a party, _____.
A. I wasn't wearing a bra
B. toilet paper was popping out of my bra
C. a hand was slipping down my bra

13. My personal party philosophy is _____.
A. arrive on time, mingle over one drink, leave early
B. arrive early, overdrink while mingling, leave late
C. arrive late, freshen drink and upgrade date (repeat if necessary), leave early the next morning

14. The baddest thing I've ever done in the hostess's bathroom is _____.
A. used her last tampon
B. popped her last Valium
C. peed, wiped with a face towel, locked the door, and passed out in the tub

15. My foolproof last-minute excuse for not making the party is _____.
A. my car broke down
B. I'm having a nervous breakdown
C. I've been attacked by a clown

Wallflower Girl

If you answered A to most questions, you're a wilting wallflower and the loaf of the party! Not good, honey. You're taking up space and boring everyone around you to tears, if they even notice you. You always play it safe at parties—and that's no way to play. Wake up! The hors d'oeuvres aren't the only things passing you by. Live a little, for Bad Girl's sake! But before you go to one more party, read this book, cover to cover, twice. And that's an order.

Budding Bad Girl

If you answered B to most questions, you are a Budding Bad Girl—and quite possibly the laugh of the party. You have excellent party growth potential and are sure to blossom into a Super Bad Party Diva with proper care, feeding, and fertilization. So get out there and celebrate yourself like you mean it. Train hard, dig deep, and go for the bad girl gold—living the Party Life every day in every way.

Super Bad Party Diva

If you answered C to most questions, congratulations! You are a Super Bad Party Diva—and the life of the party. You're not just the It girl, you're the She girl, the He girl, and the Everyone Wants to Be girl. It's no surprise you're invited to every party in town. When you make your entrance, all heads turn and the real fun begins. You spread the bad word, show the world some love, and turn every moment of your life into a celebration. You are the cultured pearl in the Bad Girl social swirl. Bless you!

Plagued Party Personas

If you're not living the Party Life of your dreams, perhaps it's your company. Watch out for these overly image-conscious plagued party personas—ditch them and replace them with genuine bad girls!

Blah-Blah Gabor

The look: Gossipy and glamorous

The attitude: Let's talk therapy, dahling.

Party line: "If you don't have anything nice to say, come sit by me."

Telltale party foul: Gossiping to you about you

Charlie's Hell's Angel

The look: Sexy, skin-tight leather and killer boots

The attitude: I like it fast and hard, like my bike.

Party line: "My body is a registered weapon and I'm aiming for action."

Telltale party foul: Riding your date on the dance floor

Doris Day-Glo

The look: Fluorescent personality and wardrobe

The attitude: I love everyone!

Party line: "I don't need booze to have fun!"

Telltale party foul: Falling hard for the secretly gay guy and making you listen to her sob story all night long

Banana Wintour

The look: Dark glasses and a darker sense of humor

The attitude: I am the fashion queen of my destiny.

Party line: "Of course it's Gucci/Prada/Dolce & Gabbana. I can't believe you have to ask."

Telltale party foul: Slipping on her haute heels and wiping out in front of the crowd

Anaïs None

The look: Distant, foreign, mysterious

The attitude: Look but do not touch.

Party line: "I don't think we've met—and that's how I like it"

Telltale party foul: Accidentally setting your hair on fire with her cigarette while picking up the cute guy you're talking to

Joan and Tom Collins

The look: Lusty, busty, and smudged

The attitude: My heart is an open bottle.

Party line: "I really, really like you and this is only my second drink."

Telltale party foul: Hitting on your date (again!)

Scandal Burnheart

The look: Naughty but haughty

The attitude: I'm so bad, I'm better than you.

Party line: "Do I know you? Do I care?"

Telltale party foul: Seducing the host, the hostess, and every other happy couple—just for conquest kicks

Party R & D

Need a little inspiration? Want a few fab tips for achieving your specific bad girl party plan? Just look to the stars—Hollywood's bad girl movie stars, that is. To learn all the right moves, all you have to do is a little Research & Development on your silver screen role model.

To seduce that younger man

Movie to rent: *The Graduate*

Bad girl to watch: Anne Bancroft

Must-use line: "Do you want me to seduce you?"

To get the spotlight you deserve

Movie to rent: *All About Eve*

Bad girl to watch: Anne Baxter

Must-use line: "Fasten your seatbelts, it's going to a bumpy night."

To out-bitch the competition

Movie to rent: *Heathers*

Bad girl to watch: Winona Ryder

Must-use line: "Heather, why are you such a mega-bitch?"

To prove your point with any arrogant, clueless man

Movie to rent: *When Harry Met Sally*

Bad girl to watch: Meg Ryan

Must-use line: "Oh, oh, ooh, ohhh, oh God, ooh, oh God, Oh, ahh, ahh, oh God, oh yeah. Right there. (gasp) (gasp) Oh, oh, oh, oh God, oh. Yes! Yes! Yes! Yes! Yes! Yes! Ah, ah, ah yes! Yes! Ah yes! Yes! Yes! Yes! Yes! Yes! Oh. Oh. Oh. Oh God. Oh."

moves in the grocery store when a good song comes on. You know it's time to

To win his heart with your charm

Movie to rent: *Breakfast at Tiffany's*
Bad girl to watch: Audrey Hepburn
Must-use line: "So listen, Fred baby—"
  "Uh, it's Paul baby."
  "Oh, is it? I thought it was 'Fred baby'"

To put your boy-toy in his place

Movie to rent: *The Ice Storm*
Bad girl to watch: Sigourney Weaver
Must-use line: "I have a husband. I don't particularly feel the need for another."

To school your boyfriend or husband in public

Movie to rent: *Who's Afraid of Virginia Woolf?*
Bad girl to watch: Elizabeth Taylor
Must-use line: "I hope that was an empty bottle,

Party Prescriptions from
Dr. Bad Girl

Your symptoms:
You're totally obsessed with a personal problem and can't think or talk about anything else.

Your bad girl cure:
 Throw a Women's Group Therapy Party!
• Gather all guests in a circle.
• Light a candle and incense.
• Take hands and feel the healing energy.
• Discuss your crisis in agonizing detail until guests solve your problem or nod off, then move on to the next patient.

leave a party when you're caught rummaging through the pantry looking for

George. You can't afford to waste good liquor, not on your salary."

To make a hunk feel appreciated
Movie to rent: *Body Heat*
Bad girl to watch: Kathleen Turner
Must-use line: "You're not too smart, are you? I like that in a man."

To voice your opinion on being single
Movie to rent: *Jezebel*
Bad girl to watch: Bette Davis
Must-use line: "This is 1852, dumplin', 1852—not the Dark Ages. Girls don't have to simper around in white just because they're not married."

To let your sexy boss know you're interested
Movie to rent: *The Sound of Music*
Bad girl to watch: Julie Andrews
Must-use line: "The Reverend Mother always says, when the Lord closes a door, somewhere he opens a window."

To turn a punishment into a party
Movie to rent: *The Breakfast Club*
Bad girl to watch: Ally Sheedy
Must-use line: "Vodka. Whenever. Tons."

To rally the troops and team-build at the office
Movie to rent: *Clockwatchers*
Bad girl to watch: Parker Posey
Must-use line: "No machine can replace me 'til everyone's had a drink. Want some?"

snacks. You know it's time to throw a party when your apartment stays neat and

Things To Do with . . . Pantyliners

* Create irresistible party invitations that guests can stick to refrigerators, computer screens, or dashboards as a friendly reminder!

* Inscribe with "Hello my name is" and distribute at corporate gatherings.

* Create personalized napkin rings for all your formal dinner parties.

* Use as beer cozies to keep your hands warm and beverages cold.

* Wear five or six as a party diaper and avoid those long bathroom lines.

* Use for last-minute bikini line cleanup for unexpected romantic encounters.

* Write "Do Not Disturb" and stick to door knob when "exploring" host's bedroom.

* Adhere to door jamb to block the lock (perfect for dorm parties and other easy-entry bashes).

* Blot cheeks after heated dancing or other sweat-inducing party activities.

* Make perfect stick-on gift cards for any occasion.

* Adhere one to each butt cheek to avoid contact with cold or unsavory toilet seats.

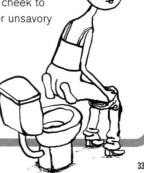

33

It's a Surprise Party!

The next time something lousy happens to you, don't throw a fit—throw an impromptu surprise party! Celebrating in the face of adversity is not only fun—it's also a great way to diffuse a bad situation and confuse the evil-doer. Keep a few impromptu party supplies in your desk, car, or purse as your personal Party Life preserver.

Impromptu Party Supplies: Bubbles, confetti, party poppers, dance moves, party horns, party hats

When Bad Things Happen to Bad Girls

The bad thing: Someone cuts you off in traffic.
What you say: "Surprise! I love you!"
What you do: Throw a fistful of confetti and blow him a kiss.

The bad thing: Your computer crashes.
What you say: "Surprise! It's a downtime again! Coffee, anyone?"
What you do: Skip down the halls blowing bubbles.

The bad thing: A meter maid is writing you a ticket.
What you say: "Surprise! It's my birthday. Thank you so much. It's just what I wanted!"
What you do: Give her a big kiss and a hug.

The bad thing: Your credit card is declined.
What you say: "Surprise! I'm a winner! Oh my God! I just won this month's spending competition!"
What you do: Pull the string on a few party poppers and run around shaking people's hands.

delay between your body and mind. You know it's time to throw a party when your

The bad thing: You get dumped.
What you say: "Surprise! I'm gay! I was just faking it anyway!"
What you do: Don a party hat and blow a party horn in his face.

The bad thing: Your boss insults you in a meeting.
What you say: "Surprise! I can't hear you. The music's too loud!"
What you do: Dance around the room and out the door.

boyfriend tells you that he "needs some space." You know it's time to leave a party

the power pre-party

The Bad Girl's Power Pre-Party can start an hour, a day, or a week before the party—or even as you're leaving your last party. You can do it alone or do it with friends. A perfect pre-party works like a pre-game warm-up. It gets you pumped up, loosened up, and ready to play your best bad girl game.

A pre-party is not about getting a buzz going early. It's about getting the bad girl fun going early.

Ms. Baddy Manners says . . . Pre-party drinking can be a sign of a serious alcohol problem. So when you do it, don't tell anyone.

Pre-party essentials:
* rallying music
* hair and makeup (or not)
* multiple outfit changes
* your bad girl alias
* your alias accessories
* face-offs in front of the mirror
* pre-party snacks

Pre-Party Rallying Tunes
Whether you're dancing half naked around your bedroom, practicing your party faces in the mirror, or psyching up in your car three blocks from the party, just pump up the volume of your favorite rallying tunes to plump up your Bad Girl party attitude.

when you wake up on the front lawn. You know it's time to throw a party when

The Warm-Up Mix

Pre-party classics sure to turn you up and on and get your booty shakin'!

Girls Just Wanna Have Fun *(Cyndi Lauper)*

I'm Coming Out *(Diana Ross)*

Flashdance: What a Feeling *(Irene Cara)*

I Love Rock 'n' Roll *(Joan Jett)*

Dancing Queen *(Abba)*

I Touch Myself *(Divinyls)*

Party Girl *(U2)*

Hot Stuff *(Donna Summer)*

We Got the Beat *(Go-Go's)*

Fight for Your Right *(Beastie Boys)*

1999 *(Prince)*

I See You Baby (Shakin' That Ass) *(Groove Armada)*

Ready or Not *(Fugees)*

Walking on Sunshine *(Katrina & the Waves)*

Let's Go *(The Cars)*

Celebration *(Kool and the Gang)*

Freedom *(George Michael)*

I Wanna Be Bad *(Willa Ford)*

Family Affair *(Mary J. Blige)*

Get Ur Freak On *(Missy Elliott)*

Good Girl Do's (Bad Girl Don'ts)

Steer clear of these girls—and their hairdos. If someone you know and love is taking her hair too seriously, step in and snip off her hair extensions and hair pretensions.

Her Hairstyle	What She Thinks It Says	What It Really Says
long and perfectly straight	I'm a classic beauty.	I'm a total snooty.
chunky highlights	I'm so Hollywood.	I'm so last season.
bleached blond	I'm more fun!	I'm more dumb!
baby pigtails	I'm crazy cute!	I'm just plain crazy.
long and wavy	My hair is a blanket of silk—go on, touch it.	My hair is my security blanket—touch it and die.
shaved head	My head symbolizes my rejection of the American beauty ideal.	I lost a bet.
pixie cut	I'm super-stylish.	I'm super-childish.

bright green, blue, or purple hair	I'm so creative you can't ignore me.	I'm so insecure and/or bored. Please notice me!
not-a-stray-hair bob	I'm totally in control.	I'm a total control freak.
a really bad dye job	I've just been to the salon.	I've just been to Wal-Mart.
perfect ringlets	I'm as sexy as Sarah Jessica Parker.	*Sex and the City* is the only sex I get.
an asymmetrical cut	I'm on the cutting edge of hair architecture.	I was so cute in the '80s!
Pebbles ponytail on top	I'm a cutie-pie hipster.	I'm over 30 but I sure wish I wasn't.
the sloppy high bun	I'm refined yet relaxed.	I have two left hands or two kids—or both.

Dial Your Style

When it's time to beauty up, don't just follow the fashion magazines, follow your wildest dreams! A blowout party is the perfect time to blow off your everyday look and try something really different. Push the limits of your bone structure—and your self image. Who knows, you may love the new bad girl you. Can't decide on tonight's look? Just close your eyes, stir your finger around in the air, and pick one of these bad girl makeup icons.

Grocery Store Checker: *paint by those everyday-low-price numbers*

Goth Girl: *that hipster cadaver look, more dead than alive*

Country 'n' Western Cutie: *super-size that hair and makeup*

Super Model: *only the latest and greatest products applied by someone else*

Drag Queen: *the larger-than-life woman you secretly want to be*

Trashy Televangelist: *tarantula eyelashes that only the Lord could love*

Cosmetics Counter Girl: *overdoing with every product known to woman*

Queen Elizabeth: *pursed lips, virgin-white powdered face, gravity-defying hair*

your best friend calls you sobbing because her boyfriend "needs some space." You

Book a Look

Having a pre-party fashion crisis? Can't decide what to wear again tonight? No problem! Just play Book a Look and turn your fashion frustration into fashion inspiration.

What you need:
* this book
* a straight shot into your closet
* a little pent-up frustration

What you do:
Open your closet door wide and sit on your bed. Then fling this book like a Frisbee into your closet—once, twice, three times in a row. Whatever falls to the floor, you get to mix and match into an outfit. No do-overs, no apologies, no more fashion anxiety!

It's All About the Attitude

Sometimes even the most experienced bad girl needs a little help slipping into and zipping up her party attitude. Start with some pump-up-your-volume music. Then begin to move until you feel the groove and find the boogie in your butt. Then get down, way down, with your bad girl self.

As you're trying on outfits, shoes, and party personas, try out a few aliases, too. The perfect alias is your personal pass to the VIP Party Life lounge and any bad girl on the party circuit knows why. It's your way in the front door, your introduction to a fabulous, inhibition-free Party Life—and it's your backdoor exit out of sticky situations that may arise from your social genius.

Instant Party Girl Alias Finder

	First Name	Last Name	Examples
Your Exotic Foreigner Name	your favorite spice	your last vacation spot	*Ginger Prague* *Curry Santa Fe* *Paprika Bali*
Your Socialite Name	your silliest childhood nickname	the town where you first partied	*Inky Austin* *Boo Mandeville* *Cammy Lafayette*
Your Fly Girl Name	your first initial	the first two or three letters of your last name	*K. Chy* *S. Be* *J. Ma*
Your Rock Star Name	any liquid on the bar	the last name of your best bad girl celebrity	*Gin Barrymore* *Brandy Jagger* *Amaretto Lopez*

Accessorizing Your Alias

Once you've selected a bad girl alias, then it's time to accessorize it for the full effect. Of course, the first accessory is always the appropriate attitude.

Exotic Foreigner Accessories

* slight accent
* fake passport
* exotic incense perfume
* luggage tag on your purse or wrist
* foreign currency sticking out of pocket
* pockets loaded with airplane-size bottles of booze
* in-flight movie headphones around neck
* dark circles under eyes for dramatic jet-lagged look
* airline pillowcase as clutch purse

Socialite Accessories

* perilously impractical shoes
* fake savage tan
* big boobs (stuff or wear a water bra if necessary)
* huge diamonds and/or pearls (fake is more authentic)
* plastic smile
* high-mileage hair in tight bun
* older (richer) man on arm
* fur or Pashmina wrap

Fly Girl Accessories

* tinted Technicolor shades
* hip huggers
* exposed midriff
* a hint of butt cleavage
* FOXY gold chain choker
* platform shoes
* DJ bag
* knee pads
* bodyguard

Rock Star Accessories

* tight faded denim
  or leather jeans or skirt
  * chunky belt
  * crimped hair
  * something snakeskin
  * go-go boots
  * guitar, tambourine, or drumsticks
  * all-access backstage pass
  * groupies
  * 12-step meeting schedule

time to leave a party when you're tongue doesn't seem to fit in your mouth anymore.

Party Etiquette

Ms. Baddy Manners says . . .

* If you don't have time to clean your bathroom—or any room—before a party, just unscrew the light-bulbs and light a few strategically placed candles. If your place is really disgusting, candles in the shapes of erotic body parts will surely distract your guests!

* When considering a party invitation, be careful not to confuse a free-booze party with a booze-free party!

* To make an overnight guest feel welcome, leave a fresh towel and a condom on the bedside table.

* Wearing white undies to a social gathering after Labor Day—party a no-no. Wearing no undies to a social gathering—party a go-go!

* When writing a thank-you note, it's best to re-create your party state of mind in order to accurately recall every fabulous party detail. So, if you were drunk at the party, get drunk to write your thank-you note. If you were naked, get naked. And so on.

The Pre-Party Snack

Never show up at a party with an empty stomach or you'll find yourself chasing down the hors d'oeuvres tray, speed-shoveling chips and dip—or worse. And without some protective padding, that first drink hits you like a ton of bricks. How can you live the Party Life when you're down for the count?

Quick, easy, high-absorbency snacks:

* peanut butter and jelly sandwich
* Pop Tart or frozen waffle
* slice of pizza
* chips or pretzels
* banana
* anything from a drive-thru window on the way
(The post-party snack = all of the above.)

The Pre-Party Pack

If you're feeling lucky, pack a Bad Girl's Party First Aid Kit in your purse before you leave.

* two tins of breath mints
  (use as mini maracas in a pinch)
* pantyliners
* travel toothbrush with paste
  pre-applied (Luck is when
  preparation meets opportunity!)
* condom (If you pack it, he will come.)
* CDs or tapes with a great Girl Power mix
* ibuprofen and/or Alka-Seltzer
* mini Bible to carry on Sunday morning walk of shame

Remember: It's badder to be safe than sorry!

to move out—and informs you that you won't be getting your security deposit back.

The Pre-Party Face-Off [A Checklist]

A bad girl is confident and prepared to handle any social situation with grace and style. Naturally, this calls for a little preparation. Before leaving the house, you and your pre-party posse must master each of these facial expressions in front of the mirror. When you've checked every box, you're good to go.

- ❏ smug, popular kid face
- ❏ lusty, seductive stare
- ❏ genuine smile
- ❏ fake smile
- ❏ real laugh
- ❏ fake laugh
- ❏ real fake laugh
- ❏ so happy to see you (not!) face
- ❏ my ex just walked in but I don't care look
- ❏ cool dance face
- ❏ sincere listener face
- ❏ concerned dog head tilt
- ❏ can you believe what that loser just said? sneak peek
- ❏ relaxed and confident adult look
- ❏ I have no idea who you are but I'll never tell nod and smile
- ❏ across the crowded room smoldering stare
- ❏ is he/she for real? secret glance
- ❏ don't even think of talking to me glare
- ❏ I'm not trashed look
- ❏ get me out of here now! face

Throwing the Party

*W*hen a bad girl throws a party, she is always the wizard of Ahh's. She knows how to host a distinctive party with tons of style, spark, and velocity—and how to make it look effortless. Whatever the mood, theme, or event, a bad girl party has it going on. The fun is firing on all social cylinders, the mix is unexpectedly spicy, the menu is inspired, and the concept is high.

Anyone can throw a party. But when a bad girl throws a party, it sticks—in your memory, in your photo album, and to your shoes. A successful bad girl bash gets everyone talking, thinking, laughing, dancing, and acting on their bad girl impulses—even the guys. Every bad girl party has a scandalous secret agenda (fun!) and it starts when the hostess pulls the right party strings.

When a bad girl hostess walks through a room, she makes waves in the crowd and ripples in the nipples around her. She glows in the dark. Guests swoon at her beauty and stutter at her style. Everyone clamors to be near, to overhear her witty words and share her rarefied high-attitude air. A bad girl hostess is the lady of the house and the Alice in her wonderland.

Party Planning Decoder
A seasoned bad girl knows that every whim, emotion, or twist of fate can justify throwing a party. Not sure how to turn a pile of dirty laundry into a fabulous fete? Just check out Your Party Planning Decoder. With the right attitude, every day can be a bad girl party.

Your Party Planning Decoder

What's Going On for You	What You Tell Yourself	What You Tell Your Friends
Your apartment is a dump and you're flat broke.	It'll be a really fun, bonding experience.	It's a pizza and painting party!
You're single—and proud of it—and sick of all your old stuff.	Gloria Steinem would so be proud.	It's a Single-Power Shower! PS: I'm registered everywhere.
Your wine rack is empty.	My friends are lucky to know someone as sophisticated as me.	It's an evening of wine tasting! All guests must bring at least three bottles, of course.
You just got a horrible haircut and you're afraid to leave the house.	It's not safe for me to be alone in this condition.	It's a Bad Hair Party!
You haven't kissed anyone in over a year.	Spin the Bottle is retro chic!	It's a Junior High Party!
You aren't meeting any strong, quality men anymore.	Maybe it's time to date strong, quality women, too.	It's the Ultimate Single Mingle!

Your therapist is on vacation for a whole month.	People who need people are the luckiest people in the world.	It's Women's Group Therapy Night!
Your divorce is finally final.	I deserve to celebrate all weekend, damn it!	It's a Marriage-Ender Bender!
Your cat brought a live rat inside your house as a loving gift—and you can't catch the thing!	I'll laugh about this when it's over.	It's a Rat-Catch Fever Party! Winner takes all!
Your skin is flawless, your weight is perfect, your bod is Hollywood hard—and you're single!	I'll never ever look this good again!	It's a Nude Year's Eve Party!
Your dearest friend is engaged to a cheating loser, a serious boozer, or a West Hollywood cruiser.	If it were me, I'd want to know before the wedding.	It's a Bridal Cold Shower!
You're moving out of your dumpy apartment and you're still broke.	It'll be a really fun, bonding experience.	It's a pizza and moving party!

the party mix

The people you invite into your Party Life are the characters in your show. If you cast them with an eye for conflict, drama, charisma, and sex appeal, you're sure to have an entertaining evening. Always start a guest list with your fab five: a friend with a great laugh, a great conversationalist, a great dancer, a great gossip, and a friend with a great sense of style. Be sure to throw in unexpected pairings—feuding siblings, ex-lovers, ex-friends, extra-brainy, extra-baked, extra-conservative, extra-gay, extra-crunchy, extra-chic—just for fun! The mix is like your appetite. It's always craving new, different things in unexpected combinations at strange times of the night.

Recommended Party Tunes

Your music stirs up the party magic. It's the soundtrack, the rhythm section, the mood ring, and the fairy dust of any good party. The music makes you and your guests move and groove, it makes you remember and feel, it makes you hot and crazy for *la vida* party. If you choose your music mix as carefully as you choose your outfit, you'll both be the life of the party. A bad girl hostess makes sure that Mr. DJ has all the right tools in his bag of party tricks.

believe you actually sound like Whitney Houston. You know it's time to throw a

Inviting Invitations

Why be predictable when you can be provocative?

Bad Good-Girl Invitations	Good Bad-Girl Invitations
message in a bottle	pantyliner in a condom
early-morning phone call	last-minute crank call
treasure map (X marks the spot!)	pleasure map (G marks the spot!)
an Evite	a Pee-vite (yellow letters in the snow)
store-bought Save the Date card	handmade Save Someone Else's Date card
forwarding party details via Interoffice Mail	forwardly whispering the details to an interoffice male
question written in the sky	question written on your thigh

Personal Party Favors

A bad girl hostess knows that the right party favor is a gift that makes her guests feel good—in all the right places. Give these empowering personal favors at your next dinner party and see how grateful your guests are for your attention to detail.

Impersonal Party Favors	Personal Party Favors
a stuffed animal	a piñata stuffed with naughty treats
a small bottle of bath bubbles	a large bottle of bubbly
a party hat and plastic party horn	a condom and plastic shoehorn
five chocolate kisses	five minutes in the closet with the hostess
edible candy necklace	edible undies
a lottery ticket	a kiss-me ticket
a mini harmonica	a mini vibrator
a disposable Polaroid camera	incriminating Polaroid photos
a tiny bottle of body glitter	a tiny bottle of lube
soap on a rope	a toy stethoscope
a pre-paid phone card	pre-paid phone sex
a tasteful blank book	this book
a small bag of hard candy	a small bag of Viagra

Do You Have Entertaining Issues?

If you have entertaining issues you haven't resolved, you could be filling your Party Life with pathological strife. Before you throw another party, take an honest inventory of your hostess habits. Then review the list below. Do any of these crappy ho' styles sound vaguely familiar? If so, then you may have a little hostessing problem. Do not despair. With a little bad behavioral therapy and the hot hostessing tips in this chapter, you'll be a happy ho' in no time!

Are You a Happy Ho' or a Crappy Ho'?

Blotto Ho' *Can't throw a party unless she's totally hammered.*

Pimpin' Ho' *Can't stop herself from setting up every single guest.*

Neuro-Perfecto Ho' *Absolutely cannot throw a party unless everything is PERFECT!*

Procrasto Ho' *Always getting into the shower when guests arrive.*

Stop-and-Go Ho' *Can't even finish a sentence before running off to start another conversation.*

Psycho Ho' *Loves her guests madly but can't stop stabbing them in the back.*

Nympho Ho' *Not satisfied until she's got hot and cold running guests in her bedroom.*

Time-to-Go Ho' *Just when her party starts rockin', she flashes the lights and tells everyone to start walkin'.*

Bordeaux Ho' *No one really enjoys her until she breathes for a while and opens up.*

Barbie Do' Ho' *So plastic and fake everyone secretly wants to rip off her perfect outfit, draw all over her with felt pens, and burn off her hair.*

to leave a party when you're having a deep conversation with yourself in the

Happy Hostess To-Do List [A Checklist]

Don't even open the door before you've checked every box on this list.

❑ Select a fab party alias.

❑ Stock up on toilet paper.

❑ Compliment self on outfit, hair, face, boobs, and butt.

❑ Stash all trashy fashion magazines and embarrassing catalogs in the washing machine and replace with the *Utne Reader, National Geographic,* and *The Economist.*

❑ Safely lock away all valuables and pets.

❑ Load the CD player with great party mood music.

❑ Practice party faces in the mirror.

❑ Repeat party mantra three times.

❑ Stash all the really good wine in the trunk of the car.

❑ Replace fat anti-snack-attack photo on the fridge with a hot, fun-loving photo of self.

❑ Flush all toilets.

❑ Check teeth for food or other crud.

❑ Eject *Buns of Steel* video, insert *Fun with Neal* home video.

❑ Invite and or/warn neighbors.

❑ Add (and cross out) "give big bucks to charity again" to to-do list by the phone.

- Bury the Preparation H, dandruff shampoo, zit cover-up, and all prescription meds at the bottom of the dirty clothes hamper.

- Make bedroom into an irresistible love lair.

- Hide self-help books and anti-teeth-grinding mouth guard under the bed.

- Light all strategically placed aromatherapy candles.

- Pull down ratty flannel jammies from hook on the bathroom door and replace with a sexy negligee.

- Do the Bad Girl Dance (see page 152) to a favorite song.

patented bad girl parties

 *The Vixen Mixen*

Every bad girl loves a naughty girl's night out—and lusts for a naughty girl's night in. The Vixen Mixen is the perfect house party when you and your foxy female friends are craving a night of open conversation, open sensuality, and open containers. Any time you're sick of the party circuit and need to stoke your inner bad girl fire, just organize a little Vixen Mixen and watch the sparks fly.

Guest List: All of the girls in your inner-baddy circle, plus any foxy girls you think are ready to cross over from good to bad

Invitations: Find a pack of X-rated male stud playing cards. Cover the dull side with a mailing label where you write the party details and each guest's name and address. Add stamps and drop the cards in the mail. (You'll also be a good citizen sharing the love with the U.S. Postal Service!)

Menu:

* Every bad girl brings her favorite secret bad indulgence food and enough forks for all.
* Plenty of good champagne or Bad Girl cocktails to lubricate the conversation

Attire: Start with your best and baddest lingerie. Finish with that super-sexy outfit you never wear in public because you always chicken out at the last minute.

Party Games: *"First and Worst" Drinking Game.* Each bad girl tells about her first kiss, sex, boyfriend and her worst kiss, sex, boyfriend. Everyone must take a sip of their

bathroom mirror. You know it's time to throw a party when you've memorized the

drink when the words "first" or "worst" are uttered.

Bad Girl Confessional Charades. Each bad girl writes her steamiest confessions on notes, folds them up, and places them in a hat. Players draw a confession from the hat and silently act out the dirty deed. The bad girl who guesses the deed correctly gets to perform the next Confessional Charade. Extra credit if she can guess the bad girl who did the deed.

I've Got a Secret! All vixens sit in a circle. One by one, each guest whispers her naughtiest secret desire to the girl next to her. Each passes the message on until it's been around the room. The last vixen announces the sinful secret. Always pee-in-your-pants hilarious!

Musical Mules. In this shoe fetishist's dream party game, play musical chairs but replace the chairs with fabulous mules—and watch your guests scramble! Find enough gorgeous pairs of mules for all but one of the players and hire a DJ to work the music, monitor the players, and break up any catfights. Arrange mules in pairs, in the center of the room. Gather guests around the chairs and have the DJ start the tunes. When the music stops, the guests dash for the most darling pair. Whoever is left mule-less must leave the game, kissing all of the remaining players' feet on the way out. The winner receives a free foot massage and pedicure at a local salon.

Party Favors: Each guest receives red lipstick, a mini vibrator, and small bottle of lube.

 *Hot-Luck Party*

Instead of bringing a favorite food dish, each guest brings her favorite hot man—and he'd better be a real dish, because he's going to be nibbled by all the bad girl guests. A Hot-Luck Party is guaranteed to serve up the bad boy and bad girl in all your guests—and get everyone's mouth watering.

Guest List: Six to eight of your favorite hungry, single bad girl friends

Invitations: In addition to the date, time, and place, request that each guest bring an available, hot man and be prepared to share.

Sample dishes:

* hot and spicy
* cool and refreshing
* healthy, fat-free
* foreign and exotic
* sweet and rich for dessert

Ms. Baddy Manners Says . . . When hosting a Hot-Luck Party, be sure to remind your guests to wrap their dish in foil or clear plastic wrap so it retains its freshness!

the hostess "Mom." You know it's time to throw a party when you just earned

Attire: A hot little outfit that whets your sexual appetite and brings you good luck—and a bib.

Party Game: *The Bad Boy Buffet.* When the hostess announces "Dinner is served," guests line up and make their way along the Bad Boy Buffet, admiring each dish, sampling with little nibbles and bites, and taking her favorites away with her to a dark corner or room. Remember: If you see a dish you really like and are about to go for it but another guest beats you to the punch, you'll just have to share. After all, that's what the Hot-Luck Party is all about.

Party Favors: Each guest receives chapstick, breath freshener, and a condom all discreetly rolled inside a linen napkin and tied with a festive bow.

Ms. Baddy Manners says . . . At a formal dinner party, always use the small salad fork when gently poking a man's rump to test for firmness.

The Truth About Drinks and Men

What He Orders	What He Thinks It Says	What It Really Says
A Bud	I'm real macho.	I'm real cheap.
Double martini, straight up	I'm Bond, James Bond.	I'm bombed, James, bombed.
Chardonnay	I'm in touch with my feminine side.	I'm a touch on the feminine side.
Margarita	I'm a fun-loving, tropical dude.	Don't go home with me unless you really want to see me hurl.
Bad Girl Cocktail	I love strong women.	I'll do anything to score a strong woman.
Tanqueray & Tonic	I'm a class act.	I'm a class-act bore.
Red Bull & Vodka	I'm ready to go all night!	It's past my bedtime.

Mineral water	My body is a temple.	I'm the designated driver, a recovered alcoholic—or both.
Long Island Iced Tea	I'm a party animal!	I'm 16!
Shot of Jack Daniels	I'm hardcore.	I'm a hardcore alcoholic.
Cosmopolitan	I'm cosmopolitan.	I'm a pretty boy.
Mojito	I'm exotic, sweet, and sexy.	I'm trendy.
Champagne	I celebrate life.	I celebrate every night I'm away from my wife.
Microbrew beer	I take my beer as seriously as fine wine.	I don't like wine yet.
Single-malt scotch	I am a connoisseur.	I went to Scotland last summer!

The Marriage-Ender Bender

Free at last! Free at last! Your divorce is finally final and it's time to celebrate your independence like a bad girl. No more deadbeat holding you back, no more dead-weight slowing you down. Whether it's your divorce or a friend's divorce, the Marriage-Ender Bender will kick off a new joyous life phase and feel as great as kicking off a pair of painful pumps at the end of a long day.

Guest List:
* Anyone who's ever gotten divorced or just wish they had
* All the men you've ever wondered about
* Your bad girl crew, who told you so but never actually said, "I told you so"
* The young, hunky construction workers from that remodel across the street

Invitations: Write party details on the back of your divorce attorney's business card. (Set up an escalating fee for every referral, in case you start a trend.) Or use up the last of your monogrammed stationery. (Cross out his name or write "Not!" next to his name.) Sign with a lip-stick kiss.

Menu:
* All the foods he hated that you were deprived of for years
* High-end bartending service featuring young, muscle-bound cupcakes serving individual bottles of expensive champagne with a straw (all on his credit card, of course)

sentence with "You know what makes me really sad . . ." You know it's time to

The Girl Power Mix

Guaranteed to unite, inspire, and ignite your collective bad girl fire:

Independent Women *(Destiny's Child)*

Bitch *(Meredith Brooks)*

Bad Reputation *(Joan Jett)*

You Oughta Know *(Alanis Morissette)*

These Boots Are Made for Walkin'
(Nancy Sinatra)

Shameless *(Ani DiFranco)*

Criminal *(Fiona Apple)*

Sisters Are Doin' It for Themselves
(Eurythmics)

Into the Fire *(Sarah McLachlan)*

No Angel *(Dido)*

I'm Every Woman *(Whitney Houston)*

No Man's Woman *(Sinead O'Connor)*

I Will Survive *(Gloria Gaynor)*

American Woman *(Lenny Kravitz)*

Bad Girls *(Donna Summer)*

Holiday *(Madonna)*

Proud Mary *(Ike & Tina Turner)*

Attire: *You wear* anything spotlighting your gorgeous, emancipated cleavage—ideally your wedding gown, cut scandalously short with a serrated edge or chainsaw. Add black fishnets, fabulous heels, and a splashy feather boa.

Your guests wear old bridesmaid dresses (or wedding gowns) torn revealingly.

Party Games:

* *Decorate the Divorcee's Car!* Scrawl "Just Divorced!" across the back window. Add "Available" and her phone number on all the side windows. Attach fun marriage mementos to rear bumper: little bride and groom figurines with nooses tied around the necks; ex-husband's shoes; ex-husband's favorite putter; ex-husband.

* *Photo-Album Fun!* Hand out your wedding and other photo albums and scissors then let everyone cut your ex from your life.

* *Pin the Ass on the Ass!* Enlarge an unflattering full-length photo of your ex-husband. Find a photo of his bare ass and make as many color copies of it as you have players. Hang the full-length photo on the wall and hand out copies of his ass. One by one, each player is blindfolded. Whoever pins the ass on the ass in the funniest spot wins!

Party Favors: Each guest receives White-Out to remove his name or unsightly initials, small sewing scissors to cut him from all photos, and a can of his shaving cream to decorate the divorcee's car.

throw a party when you think your vibrator might be contributing to the energy

The Payback Party

It's just not polite to take and take from the party bowl and never give back, is it? Every now and then, say once or twice a year, a smart, savvy bad girl will organize an event that covers all bases, to thank those who need thanking and keep in touch with all who need touching. It's a bit calculated, and a bit contrived, but aren't all social events?

Guest List: Invite all of the people you owe social thanks to, but don't really want to see or talk to. Dig deep. The point is to get all of this miscellaneous socializing over with in one night. Your friend's cousin who passed your resume on? Invite her. Your old college roommate's younger sister who just moved to town whom you promised to call? Invite her. The guy from the office who you keep making and breaking lunch plans with? Invite him. You get the picture. Special Note: The more people you can invite, the better.

Be sure that a minimum of 10 guests RSVP in the positive, otherwise you will be stuck talking to people you'd rather not talk to, defeating the purpose.

Invitations: When sending invitations, write a quick, personal note on each: "It's been too long. Can't wait to catch up!" Or, "Looking forward to seeing you—I've missed you!" Or simply, "Finally!" Also, be sure to specify on the invitation that it's a cocktail party (no food means lower overhead).

Menu: When guests call ahead to see if they can bring anything, be sure to say "Oh no, no, it's all taken care of." When they reply, "Are you sure?" You say, "Oh, well, you

67

can always bring a bottle of wine if you want, but don't feel like you have to!" This ensures that at least every other guest will bring a bottle of wine, hence cutting down on overhead.

Party Game: The night of the party, it is your job to play the smiling, effervescent hostess who is neither here nor there. Always running off to check on this or that. Stash a few magazines or catalogs and a flashlight in the bathroom or a closet so you can slip off for some light reading. Plan to organize your closet so that you can disappear off into the bedroom to do something mysterious, the way hostesses often do. Before you know it, the night will be over, everyone will have had a blast, and you will be paid up through next year.

Tips to Keep It Cheap

* Buy jumbo bottles of cheapo booze and a few packs of Kool-Aid—be sure to mix the punch before guests arrive.
* Go through your cabinets and find old boxes of stale crackers, pretzels, and cereal. Toast them on a baking sheet until lightly browned, then dump it all into a big bowl or basket. Add peanuts from your 10-year collection of free airline nuts and crusty Parmesan cheese from the can at the back of the fridge and—voilà!—you've got a kicky Payback Party Mix.
* Call it a "shots party" and eliminate the need for expensive mixers and large plastic cups.
* If you have any Halloween candy left over, arrange in candy dishes around the room. If not, at least offer a bowl of breath mints or Tic-Tacs.

alcohol than you have. You know it's time to throw a party when your "new" sexy

The Scrappy Birthday Bash

How do you make every birthday party unique, hysterical, and memorable? You get scrappy, of course! Just pull your Baddy crew together and build a scrapbook shrine to the birthday girl's year of bad behavior. You'll not only laugh your way though the party, you'll also have a lasting record of a year in her life.

Guest List: Invite your core group of bad girl buddies, plus a few wild cards who may have special access to the birthday girl's life (an old friend, a cool relative, a beloved co-worker).

Invitations: Ask all the guests to dig into stacks of photos, overstuffed drawers, and email inboxes (photocopy list on next page and enclose with invitation). Their mission: to find funny, endearing, and incriminating scraps from the past year of her bad girl life. The badder the better!

Menu: Stock up on truth-serum-like beverages, plus the birthday girl's favorite foods. Gather a big scrapbook or photo album with full-page clear sleeves, and all the right

69

Things to Collect and Commemorate

* photos (the good, the bad, and the ugly)

* fortune cookie fortunes

* names of secret crushes

* obsessions

* favorite books, movies, TV shows, songs

* cocktail napkins with phone numbers, notes that make no sense, doodles

* credit card receipts from retail therapy sessions

* unpaid parking tickets

* airplane boarding passes

* concert ticket stubs

* love letters

* promises (broken)

* late bill notices

* business cards collected in bars

* snapshots of dents in her car

* locks of hair (from her, her many men—and her pet)

* defiant proclamations surreptitiously recorded after family gatherings, drinking binges, and blind dates

* transcripts from drunken voice messages

* photos of tragic fashion trends she tried to emulate

* ice-cream pint lids

* loser lottery tickets

* account balances from the ATM

scrappy tools, like glitter glue pens, gel pens, pantyliners for make-your-own stickers, glitter, yarn, glue, double-sided tape, dried flowers, fine black pens for writing all-the-dirt descriptions, and red wine and wine glasses to make burgundy rings around faces. Cover a large table with butcher paper to protect it against glue, tape, uncontrolled coloring spasms, spilled wine, and tears from uncontrolled laughter and embarrassment.

Party Game: Build the scrapbook, incriminating item after incriminating item. Be sure to have everyone at the party sign the last page.

The Scrappy Bash—
it's not just for birthdays anymore!
Turn any of the following events into a Scrapbookers' Ball of Fame, and you'll be a hostess with the mojo-ness and the envy of all your friends.

Vacation reunions *(Re-create the adventure—perfect when you can't afford to travel this year!)*

Graduation parties *(Relive the glory days and/or the embarrassment—perfect when you can't believe who you've actually become!)*

Bachelorette parties *(Memorialize her single life so she'll never forget how irreverent and fun she used to be!)*

Baby showers *(Memorialize her pre-mommy life so she'll never forget how intelligent and thin she used to be—and how much time she used to have!)*

71

 *Bad Taste Party*

This is your chance to embrace and honor all things bad, ranging from bad hair and bad manners to bad timing and a bad week.

Guest List: Anyone who's recently had a bad day, a bad date, bad luck, or all of the above

Invitations: Ugly Christmas cards purchased from the bargain bin at Wal-Mart, with "Merry Christmas" crossed out and party details scribbled in. Be sure to point out that it's a BYOB (and TP) affair.

Decor:
* Plastic covers on all furniture
* Porcelain figurines of gnomes, cows, or anything else you can find
* A stack of stolen cocktail napkins in the bathroom in place of TP
* Green indoor-outdoor throw rugs
* Ashtrays that need emptying
* Bug zapper and/or fly strip hanging over the buffet table
* Any "art" that involves black velvet, kittens, or inspirational messages

Attire: Bad fashion options should be once-upon-a-time trendy. Think cat-print sweaters, paisley pants, polyester leisure suits, or super-tight stretch pants for creating the perfect camel toe.

Bad makeup techniques include putting on lipstick outside the lines or on teeth, and applying poorly matched or poorly applied zit concealer.

to throw a party when you have zero new messages. You know it's time to leave a

Bad hair options include greasy, frizzy, messy, feathered, seriously hairsprayed, badly dyed, or 12-hour bed hair.

Party Game: *Bad Game.* The first rule of this game is that guests must behave badly. (Show up way early. Simultaneously brag and complain. Eat off of other people's plates. Stare, point, and laugh at other guests. Loudly ask specifics on salary, weight, and other intimate details.) Any well-behaved, well-spoken, or well-dressed guest will be ejected.

The second rule is that guests cannot agree on how to play the game. Bickering, interrupting, rudeness, and insisting on your rules scores points. When everyone is disgusted and walks away, the game is over and everyone wins.

Party Favors: Upon arrival, each guest receives a whole garlic clove and a cup of burnt coffee to ensure especially bad breath. When leaving, guests get cheese in a can.

party when there are three people left—you, the host, and her boyfriend. You know

Baddy Awards Night

Every year, Hollywood rolls out the red carpet, honoring the best and the brightest. Meanwhile, bad girls everywhere gather for their very own ceremony—the annual Baddy Awards, when the year's baddest girls win glorious golden shoes! Hold the event on Academy Awards night or choose your own special date. Anytime you're feeling the need to honor your badness is the right time for the Baddy Awards.

Invitations: Gold spray-painted pantyliners with fancy lettering—hand-delivered, of course. Be sure to enclose a baddy ballot with three to five nominees in each category and a brief, juicy description of each bad girl's award-worthy behavior.

Categories to consider:

* Best Bad Girl Actress in a Romantic Comedy
* Best Bad Girl in a Supporting Bra
* Best Bad Girl Drama Queen
* Best Bad Girl Director of Other People's Lives
* Best Bad Girl Costume
* Best Bad Girl Original Kiss-Off Letter
* Best Bad Girl Theme Song

Attire:

* Fabulously formal full-length gowns
* Plenty of camera-ready black mascara (it runs so dramatically when you weep)

Prep Work: Gather a wild collection of bad-girl-worthy shoes, mules, and boots from thrift stores, garage sales, or the way-back of your closet. Drench each shoe with gold spray paint, adding glitter, confetti, colored sprinkles, and anything else that lends pizzazz. Let the shoes dry for at least 24 hours.

Decor:

* Long red carpet (or a few red beach towels will do)
* Drape all seating with glamorous jewel-toned velvet
* Position the podium in front of a glitzy backdrop (glittery shower curtain, foil, or plastic wrap)

Ceremony: During every Academy Awards commerical break, your designated emcee jumps up and works the crowd, then introduces last year's winner (and her bad girl accomplishment), who then presents this year's winner. When each Baddy Award winner is announced, she must kiss and hug everyone around her, traipse to the podium, and deliver a quivering, long-winded, teary speech in which she thanks God, her parents, her agent, and everyone she's ever met.

Every girl nominated for Best Bad Girl Theme Song must perform a live karaoke version, ideally with backup singers and dancers.

You know it's time to leave a party when you're eating Cheerios dipped in picante

The Self-Pity Party

You've just been fired, dumped, arrested, evicted. You're having a bad hair month. You haven't had a date this year—or this decade. Or maybe you're just feeling like an overall pathetic loser! Whatever the source, don't suppress your pain—celebrate it! Why put on a happy face, pretending you're fine, when you can indulge your misery and wallow in your despair in the company of good friends? Even bad girls get the blues, they just do it with style and humor.

Guest List: Anyone you know or have ever met whose life is fantastic (if no one shows up, even better!)

Invitations: Pathetic, tear-stained note scrawled on the back of a parking ticket, bank balance, letter of rejection, or I'm-dumping-you email

Decor: Messy apartment, unmade bed, piles of dirty laundry, shades pulled down, burned-out lightbulbs, three days of dishes in the sink, pots on the stove with dried, crusty food, slipper-size dust bunnies in all corners

Create a shrine to your pathetic existence featuring photographs of anyone who's ever humiliated you or done you wrong (ex-boyfriends, parents, bosses, popular girls), then line up all of your school photographs, displaying your long history of bad luck, bad style, bad haircuts, prom photos, and driver's license pictures. Finish with all of your current loser life souvenirs—pink slips, moving violations,

BBQ sauce. You know it's time to throw a party when your body glitter has dried

The Pity Party Mix

Tragic tunes so sad—or so bad—that you can't help bursting into tears:

Love Bites *(Def Leppard)*

Achy Breaky Heart *(Billy Ray Cyrus)*

Ironic *(Alanis Morissette)*

Lonesome Me *(Neil Young)*

Sad Songs *(Elton John)*

Love Hurts *(Everly Brothers)*

Guess I'll Hang My Tears Out to Dry
(Linda Rondstadt)

Alone *(Moby)*

Love Stinks *(J. Geils Band)*

At Seventeen *(Janis Ian)*

Sorry I Am *(Ani DiFranco)*

Yesterday *(The Beatles)*

Everybody Hurts *(REM)*

Break Your Heart *(Barenaked Ladies)*

The Other Woman *(Nina Simone)*

Cry Me a River *(Diana Krall)*

So Far Away *(Carole King)*

Can't Smile Without You *(Barry Manilow)*

Goodbye to Love *(Carpenters)*

When It Hurts So Bad *(Lauryn Hill)*

All By Myself *(Celine Dion)*

hideous candid photos, bank balance, dry cleaning receipts for clothes you can't afford to pick up, that joyous wedding announcement of your ex and your ex–best friend.

Menu:

* 12 pints of Chubby Hubby ice cream (Eat from the carton.)
* Tortilla chips, Cheese Doodles, and a five-gallon can of caramel corn (Serve in the bag or tin.)
* Large batch of brownies (Eat directly from the pan.)
* Tube of pre-made cookie dough (Nibble all night like it's a big banana.)

up. You know it's time to leave a party when you love everyone—and tell them one

* Shots of tequila (It's too much effort to make Margaritas.)
* Wine with screw-off top (Who has the energy to find a corkscrew?)
* Diet Coke

Attire: *You wear* sweatpants and a grungy T-shirt, or any clothes that are way too tight because you've put on "a few" pounds.

Your guests wear something fabulous to make you feel even worse.

Special Touches:
* Dried cat vomit on carpet
* Sylvia Plath book on the back of the toilet
* Internet articles on "How to Disappear and Create a Whole New Identity" taped to refrigerator

Party Games: *Speed Eating Decathlon!* Select ten different food items (pint of ice cream, Slim Jim, wedge of Brie, jalapeno pepper, bag of chips . . .) Each competitor is judged on speed and quantity of consumption.

Spin the Drano Bottle! You spin the bottle and the person it lands on gets to insult you or tell you one more reason why your life sucks.

When guests want to pity themselves too, play *The Circle of Pity!* Everyone sits in a circle and one by one proclaims, "Hi, my name is _____ and I'm a pitiful loser. Here is my story." Whoever tells the most pathetic story wins—and gets to spend three minutes in the closet with Ben and Jerry!

Party Favor: Each guest receives a lovely box of candy—with a bite taken out of each piece.

by one. You know it's time to throw a party when your diaphragm has fossilized.

The Ultimate Single Mingle

If you and way too many of your male and female friends are single, don't act shy, act sly. Address the problem head-on by throwing the Ultimate Single Mingle, the party that makes it way okay to be openly looking for love. You'll increase your chances of connecting—without the risk of inbreeding with friends! Plus, you'll be amazed by how many people will join in and thank you for getting personal.

Guest List: Ten of your coolest single guy friends and ten of your coolest single girlfriends, ideally from different walks of your life and your friends' lives (Each of these guests must bring two single friends or they will not be admitted to the party.)

Menu: Inhibition-lowering beverages and light hors d'oeuvres that are easy to nibble and digest and won't get stuck in your teeth (no spinach, chives, garlic, poppy seeds, or beans)

Ms. Baddy Manners says . . . To counteract a red wine spill, spill a similar vintage white wine directly on the spot, then suck dry.

Attire: Dress for seduction success. Be sure to wear something with a pocket to hold your stash of business cards and scribbled-on matchbooks and cocktail napkins.

You know it's time to leave a party when you ask someone, "Are you pregnant or

Party Game: *Party Favors.* All guests receive a Party Favor card and a pencil. Each card has a list of six favors to be asked of different guests—people they don't already know.

Would you kindly do me the favor of . . .
* telling me your favorite joke
* dancing with me
* explaining our country's Middle Eastern foreign policy
* giving me a tour of the house
* introducing me to your cutest, sexiest friend
* confessing your latest sin
* describing the last book you read
* swapping clothes with me
* giving me your email address
* giving me your phone number
* giving me a free sample hug
* acting out a scene from your favorite movie
* teaching me your best party trick
* revealing your most successful pickup line
* describing your perfect third date

When one guest does a party favor for another, he or she then initials the card and the cardholder gives the guest a kiss of thanks. Every guest with a completed Party Favor card will be entered in a raffle to win a free dinner at a romantic restaurant with the date of his/her choice. (Hey, it's a small price to pay for getting 30 single guys to your party!)

Party Favor: A Binaca blast

just fat?" You know it's time to throw a party when your neighbors say hi to you in

The Make-Out Mix

Seductive songs to spread an epidemic of love through the crowd:

Physical *(Olivia Newton-John)*

Damn, I Wish I Was Your Lover
(Sophie B. Hawkins)

Take a Chance on Me *(Abba)*

I Know What Boys Like *(The Waitresses)*

Do You Wanna Touch Me *(Joan Jett)*

What's Love Got to Do with It *(Tina Turner)*

Like a Virgin *(Madonna)*

Hit Me with Your Best Shot *(Pat Benatar)*

I Just Wanna Make Love to You *(Etta James)*

What It Feels Like for a Girl *(Madonna)*

I Kissed a Girl *(Jill Sobule)*

Sugar Walls *(Sheena Easton)*

Flower *(Liz Phair)*

Let's Talk About Sex *(Salt-n-Pepa)*

Kiss *(Prince)*

I Want You to Want Me *(Cheap Trick)*

It Ain't Over till It's Over *(Lenny Kravitz)*

**Lady Marmalade (Voulez-Vous Coucher
Avec Moi Ce Soir)** *(Labelle)*

The Look of Love *(Diana Krall)*

sexy party games

Liven up any party with some bad girl upgrades of traditional party games.

Musical Lap Dances

Traditional musical chairs with an X-rated, hip-gyrating spin.

What you need:

* enough sturdy folding chairs for all but one player
* dimly lit room with strobe light or disco ball
* sexy, suggestive music
* sexy party guests with exhibitionist tendencies
* Polaroid camera
* DJ to work the music, monitor the players, and capture the lap dances on film

What you do:

Arrange the chairs in a double row, back to back, in the center of the room. Gather the guests and start the music. Players strut, shimmy, and shake their way around the chairs.

When the music is stopped, everyone scrambles for an empty chair. Whoever is left chairless is required to give a sexy lap dance to the nearest seated person before leaving the game.

Remove a chair after each round and continue playing until only one chair and two players remain. Whoever snags the last chair receives the final seductive lap dance and a one-month cable subscription to the Spice Channel.

Pass the Ice Cube

A chilling and thrilling way to get things moving.

What you need:

* a tray or two of fully frozen ice cubes
* bad girls
* guys who can't believe their good luck

What you do:

Ask the guests to form a circle—boy, girl, girl, girl, boy, boy, girl, boy—or something like that (definitely not boy, girl, boy, girl).

Crack the ice cube tray and place a cube in your mouth.

Without using your hands or anything else, pass the cube to the player next to you, who must then pass it to the next player, all without using hands.

Try to get the ice cube around the full circle without it—or any of the players—melting first.

If a player drops a cube, he or she must leave the game and chew ice furiously in the corner.

When only three players remain, the rest of the group should turn off the lights and tiptoe quietly out of the room. (The remaining three are, obviously, the winners.)

Bobbing for Keys

A swinging combination of the classic children's party game and the popular '70s "Key Party" theme.

What you need:

* car keys
* floatable foam key chains (sold at nautical and sporting goods stores)
* silky scarves

rollerblading at 8:00 the next morning. You know it's time to throw a party when

Party of One

Just because you're home alone doesn't mean you can't get a taste of the party life.

Movie Star Boyfriend Date

When your real boyfriend is out of town, working late on a big project, or a figment of your imagination, rent all the best movies starring your movie star man. Pour yourself a cup of tea or a glass of wine and curl up on the sofa in a sexy negligee. By the end of the evening, you'll feel so close to him that you'll be practicing signing your name joined with his—or practicing something else all by yourself.

Frisky Risky Business Bash

Imagine that you're auditioning for *Fame, Flashdance, Footloose, A Chorus Line, Billy Elliot, Showgirls,* or whatever floats your skirt. Then crank the tunes and dance around your apartment in your underwear, ideally in front of the mirror. Start with a lot of self-love, then throw in a little self-lust. You'll have happy feet, happy butt, happy hips, and a happy head in no time! After you've worked up a good sweat, cool down with a cold beverage and an erotic ice cube rubdown.

Manic Attack Purge Party

Collect a bunch of empty garbage bags and boxes and drink a strong cup of coffee. Then load all of your favorite fast dance tunes into the CD player, hit play, and pump up the volume. When you're moving with the high-speed grooving, start frantically cleaning out your closets, drawers, fridge, and anything else you haven't had the time or courage to tackle. Do not move any slower than the beat and do not stop to think. When it's all over, you won't remember a thing except the buzz—but you'll have a spotless place.

* large metal tub filled with water (large cooler, bucket, or bathtub will suffice)
* swinging guests with wet, wandering eyes

What you do:

Ask half of your guests to attach their new floatable key chains to their keys and drop them in the tub of water.

Using silky scarves, blindfold the other half of your guests and secure their hands behind their backs.

Have blindfolded players get down on their knees and, using only their mouths and teeth, bob for keys!

When a player emerges from the tub with a foam key chain clenched between his or her teeth, the owner of the keys must come forward, claim the keys, and take the lucky blindfolded bobber for a drive.

Truth or Bare

A naughty soul- and/or butt-baring version you never dared to play in high school.

What you need:
* intimate group of friends with dirty secrets, hazy histories, and everything to hide
* therapist on call

What you do:

Gather friends.

The host kicks off the game by choosing someone in the circle and posing the question, "Truth or Bare?" followed by a provocative loaded question (e.g., "Truth or Bare? Did you really fool around with that Rent-a-

your unwanted houseguest mentions that she hates parties. You know it's time

Wrangler cowboy stripper the night of your bachelorette party?" Or, "Truth or Bare? Did you really get arrested for indecent exposure last weekend when you were rolling around buck-naked with that guy on your roof?").

The player who's been asked the question must then decide what to reveal—the truth or some skin. If the question is just too much, the player should opt for "bare" instead of "truth," at which point the asker gets to choose an item of clothing for the player to remove.

After the player has either answered the question or removed an item of clothing, he or she gets to choose the next victim and ask the next question.

The game goes on and on until all players are completely exposed—both literally and figuratively—and really ready to party, since there's nothing left to lose!

Strip Twister
A racy, twisted version of the Milton Bradley game.

What you need:
* original version of Twister
* flexible group of party players who aren't afraid to get down and dirty

What you do:
Offer showers and clean towels to anyone smelling a little ripe.

Lay out the Twister mat and choose a referee to spin the wheel. When the dial lands on "left foot" and "red," for example, the first player must place his or her left foot on a red circle.

The ref continues to spin the wheel as players place hands and feet in different colored circles until they are tangled up in knots.

Anytime a player falls or touches the mat with anything other than a hand or foot, he or she must remove an item of clothing (chosen by the referee) and play on.

Once a player is completely nude, he or she must leave the game. The player who is left standing in a wacky, contorted position while all the other nude players have gone off—wins! (Or loses, depending on how you look at it.)

To raise the stakes, spritz players and the mat with a mist of flavored olive oil!

Party Game Tip

Just put the word "naked" before any traditional game or the phrase "in bed" after (e.g., Naked Charades, Pumpkin Carving in Bed, Naked Limbo Dancing, Risk in Bed, etc.) and let the games begin!

know it's time to throw a party when you start having "private jokes" with your

Party of Two

When it's just you and your long-term beau/hubby/companion again, get some short-term thrills.

Come As You Aren't Party
Instead of dinner and a movie again, throw yourself an intimate Come As You Aren't Costume Party to stir up those secret sexual fantasies and deep-seated desires. Explore roles that are totally opposite of normal, every-night you. Try authority figures (police officer, librarian, gym teacher, CEO-oh-oh!) or play rivals and renegades (cowboy and Indian, good cop/bad cop, popular kid and angry art student). Being passive-aggressive has never been so much fun! Pump up the erotic volume, and come as you aren't!

Flashback Bash
Whether you started dating ten months ago or ten years ago, a live-action flashback from your early dating days will re-ignite your relationship fire. Reenact your first date, right down to the food, footwear, and faux pas. Or repeat your first dance, good-night kiss, full-on make-out session, and so on. When you get your head back to the days and ways of raw relationship excitement, your body soon will follow.

Party of Three

Blend a Party of One with a Party of Two, add a pinch of bad, then stir until frothy. If you're the Party of Two, invite a hot one to spice up your private party mix. If you're the Party of One, invite a cool pair with moves you admire and want to study intimately. (When in doubt, use an alias!)

theme parties

Junior High Party

Spin the Bottle is retro chic! You'll be locking lips with anyone and everyone in no time!

Guest list: All the hunks, babes, and total foxes you know (Be sure to mix it up with jocks, stoners, and brains.)

Invitations: Scribble notes on blue-lined, three-hole punch notebook paper:

My parents are going to Vegas this weekend. Party at my house! [Don't forget to dot the i's with circles and hearts!]

Luv Ya,
[Insert Your Name]
Pass it on!

Decor:
* All overhead lights turned off
* Strategically placed lava lamps
* Drape the furniture with tapestries and stuff mothballs under the cushions to re-create the ambiance of a moldy basement or rec room
* Stash beanbag chairs and sleeping bags in the darkest corners
* Empty bottle for spinning

Mood Music: Glory Days Mixes (see page 92)

Menu: Bud or Schlitz in a can and whatever else you drank in junior high. Try wine coolers and peach schnapps, and disgusting concoctions of a variety of hard stuff (as if stolen from the parents' liquor cabinet) and poured into one large, anonymous container.

Attire: Whatever you wore in junior high. If you were in seventh grade in the '70s, feather your hair and bust out your bellbottoms. If you were in eighth grade in the '80s, break out your acid-wash jeans, concert T-shirts, and frosted lip gloss. If you were in ninth grade in the '90s, you should probably just skip to another party—this might be too close for comfort.

Party Games:
* *Chase and Tackle!* The perfect ice breaker that gives every guest a chance to grab and casually grope without that annoying conversation stuff.
* *Spin the Bottle.* Now that you're a bad girl, if it lands on another girl, you've gotta kiss her. Same goes for the boys.
* *30 Minutes in the Closet.* Since you're older, it takes a lot longer.
* *Truth or Truth.* Forget the dare, the truth is so much more interesting and entertaining.
* *Time Share 'rental Unit.* Rent the "parents'" bedroom for 30-minute blocks to fund more beer runs.

Party Favor: Everyone leaves with a hickey on the neck!
Ms. Baddy Manners says . . . If you don't get a neck hickey from another guest, give one to yourself!

You know it's time to throw a party when Friday night becomes laundry night.

Glory Days Mixes

'60s Mix. Whip out the beads, boots, mini skirt, or debutante bouffant.

Aquarius (Let the Sun Shine In)
(The Fifth Dimension)

Twist & Shout *(The Beatles)*

I Got You (I Feel Good) *(James Brown)*

The Twist *(Chubby Checker)*

Shout *(Dynatones)*

Louie, Louie *(Kingsmen)*

The Loco-Motion *(Little Eva)*

Do Wah Diddy Diddy *(Manfred Mann)*

Groovin' *(Rascals)*

I Got You Babe *(Sonny & Cher)*

The Kids Are Alright *(The Who)*

Build Me Up Buttercup *(The Foundations)*

I'm a Believer *(The Monkees)*

Somebody to Love *(Jefferson Airplane)*

'70s Mix. Rekindle your love of tight polyester, big hair, chunky gold chains, and glorious disco.

The Hustle *(Van McCoy)*

Night Fever *(Bee Gees)*

I Love the Nightlife *(Alicia Bridges)*

Dancing Queen *(Abba)*

Dance to the Music *(Sly and the Family Stone)*

That's the Way I Like It
(K.C. and the Sunshine Band)

Disco Inferno *(Trammps)*

YMCA *(Village People)*

Heart of Glass *(Blondie)*

Funky Town *(Lipps Inc.)*

If I Can't Have You *(Yvonne Elliman)*

Turn the Beat Around *(Vicki Sue Robinson)*

Jive Talkin' *(Bee Gees)*

Midnight at the Oasis *(Maria Muldaur)*

'80s Mix. Revive the power without getting an asymmetrical haircut or waiting to get past the velvet rope.

Wake Me Up *(Wham)*

Baby Got Back *(Sir Mix-a-lot)*

Red, Red Wine *(UB40)*

Little Red Corvette *(Prince)*

Maneater *(Hall & Oates)*

Centerfold *(J. Geils Band)*

Down Under *(Men At Work)*

The Tide Is High *(Blondie)*

Jack & Diane *(John Cougar Mellencamp)*

Do You Really Want to Hurt Me
(Culture Club)

Walk Like an Egyptian *(Bangles)*

Thriller *(Michael Jackson)*

I Want to Know What Love Is *(Foreigner)*

Say You Say Me *(Lionel Richie)*

Brick House *(Commodores)*

Retro Airline Party

Looking for a fun, unique dinner party that won't crash your food budget for the month? Try a Retro Airline Party, an evening that harkens back to the good old days when flying was about high times, glamour, and adventure!

Guest List: Anyone who claims to remember the good old days, or who can't resist the appeal of a uniform

Invitations: Make mock boarding passes that specify Coach or First Class (no e-tickets in those days). Any guests who show up with a Pan Am vinyl flight bag get an automatic upgrade.

Prep Work: Ask friends (ideally size-six girls and gay boys) to be your stewards and stewardesses (no flight attendants in those days). They will help serve drinks, dinner, and attend to your guests' every need. Obtain vintage plastic wings pins and standard 1960s polyester uni-

forms (just add colored tape trim to any dark fitted suit) for your retro airline co-hosts. They can wear their own perfect hair, perfect makeup, and plastic smiles.

Decor: Set up a karaoke microphone as in-flight intercom system so you can verbally abuse passengers, point out boring landmarks, and make really stupid jokes.

Borrow a camping porta-potty and set it up in a cramped shower stall. (Be sure to install a smoke detector.)

You know it's time to leave a party when someone asks "How are you?" and

When anyone goes into the bathroom, announce imminent turbulence over the in-flight intercom, and insist that everyone return to their seats immediately.

Mood Music: Pre-recorded soundtrack of crying babies, snoring, wheezing old men, coughing sickly passengers, crashing thunderstorms, etc.

Menu: First-class guests enjoy Hello Kitty–sized servings of grilled salmon, rice, diced vegetables, and a diced iceberg salad while seated comfortably at the dining room table. Of course, you offer complimentary chilled cheap Chardonnay and follow with fresh-baked cookies warm from the oven. (Be sure the guests in Coach can smell the baked cookies. Naturally, you firmly deny their pleas for a cookie.)

Coach guests must wedge together on the sofa to dine on mini bags of peanuts or pretzel mix and pay for all alcoholic beverages. The watery instant coffee is free!

Special Touches: Rigorous security consists of a wink, a smile, and a casual pat-down. (Feel free to conduct a full-body frisk on any suspiciously cute guests.)

Party Games: Show an in-flight movie (preferably a crappy film everyone has already seen). Be sure to pass out extra blankets to conceal in-flight hanky-panky among drunken fliers.

Party Favors: Coach guests receive mini bottles of booze, mini bags of peanuts, and plastic wings.

First-class guests get to go home with a stewardess or steward.

you actually tell them. You know it's time to throw a party when you can't

Things to Do with . . . Lemon Wedges

* Spritz behind each ear for last-minute citrus perfume (also works great with oranges and limes!).

* Bite and suck to cover cigarette breath, garlic breath, or heavy breathing.

* Slip into mouth of a cute guy with bad breath.

* Spritz above toilet to freshen up foul bathroom odors—yours or someone else's.

* Accidentally squirt in the eye of an annoying pursuer ("Oops!").

* Squirt in your own eye to get attention or an excuse to leave immediately.

* Soak in vodka and squirt in hair for sun-kissed highlights. (Pour lemon-infused vodka over ice and enjoy!)

* Rub around rim of mouth and dip lips in sugar for sweet, memorable kisses.

* Suck wedges to get saliva flowing for zesty make-out session.

* Eat entire wedge to prove how tough you are.

    * Rub vigorously on fingers to remove tobacco odor and other fishy or foul smells from fingers.

* Load into cocktail for quick vitamin C boost (justifies what others may call "problem drinking").

think of an alternative to working late. You know it's time to leave a party when

Fake Bake Party

It's the dead of winter and your skin is whiter than a dead fish. What do you do to boost morale among your bad girl and bad boy friends? Host a Fake Bake Party, of course! By the end of the evening, everyone will be golden bronzed, relaxed, and ready for anything.

Guest List: Everyone you know—except people with a real tan from a recent vacation or a perma-tan from a tanning salon

Invitations: Stroll into a travel agency and grab fistfuls of brochures for luxury beachfront resorts in steamy tropical locales. Insert your Fake Bake Party details.

Decor: Set up beach lounge chairs, umbrellas, hammocks, and sand chairs. Collect sand from beach and sprinkle over hardwood floors. Crank up the heat, turn on the humidifier, and set up fans throughout your home (extra points for ceiling fans—très tropical).

Mood Music: Play "ocean sounds" CD on stereo, while simultaneously playing steel drums or Hawaiian music cassette on boom box.

the host starts turning out all the lights and brushing her teeth. You know it's time

Menu:

* Whole coconuts, papayas, mangoes, pineapples, and machetes left around your apartment to create authentic fresh-from-the-tree island feel
* A couple dozen live crabs set free in apartment for guests to catch and boil
* Piña Coladas with mini umbrellas
* Mai Tais served in coconut shells

Attire: You and your bad girl guests wear bikini tops and sarongs (swim trunks or Speedos for the guys). Everyone goes barefoot and wears sunglasses. Encourage guests to spritz with coconut-scented oil and accessorize with sunglasses, puka shell necklaces, snorkels, masks, and

to throw a party when you feel the boogie in your butt. You know it's time to leave

beach-towel wraps. As the host, you should apply fast-acting fake tanning lotion the morning of the party so you'll be sporting a golden bronze tan when guests arrive, inspiring them to join you on your own private island.

Special Touches:
* Fill spray bottles with ocean water and spritz on guests' faces as they walk in the front door.
* Simmer coconut milk on the stove and scatter open containers of suntan oil throughout apartment.

Party Games: *Fake Bake!* When guests arrive, they must go directly to the "tanning booth" (a bathroom or bedroom will do) where sexy, savage-tanned island boys and girls slather them with fast-acting fake tanning lotion. Guests then relax in lounge chairs where they will be served Piña Coladas while the fake tanner takes action. At the end of the party, guests compete for best tan lines, worst color tan, and strangest striped pattern.

Midnight Skinny Dipping! Fill the bathtub with cool water, aqua food coloring, and salt. Turn off the lights, turn on a wave-sound machine, light papaya-scented candles, and encourage midnight skinny-dipping.

Party Favors: Puka shell necklaces and mini cocktail umbrellas

a party when you remember some old breakdancing moves and decide to show

Prom Party

Here's your chance to relive your prom night triumphs and tragedies with a healthy dose of bad girl style.

Guest List: Anyone who has suffered through a high school prom and anyone who skipped it (basically, everyone you know)

Invitations: A hokey theme (e.g., Midnight at the Oasis, Two Tickets to Paradise, Never Tear Us Apart, Stairway to Heaven) written in glue and sprinkled with glitter

Decor:
* Clear your biggest room of all the furniture. Line one wall with folding chairs, cold and hard enough to discourage necking. Along another wall set up a banquet table covered with any on-sale colored paper tablecloth.
* String crepe paper streamers from the corners of the ceiling.
* Hang a mirrored disco ball above the dance floor and aim a few spotlights or flashlights at it.
* Set up a prom photo station with a cheesy background (fake sunset, tropical island motif).

Mood Music: See Glory Days Mixes on pages 92–93.

Menu:
* A hideous buffet of rolled-up cold cuts
* Spiked Hawaiian Punch

Attire: *Girls* wear thrift-store formals or bad prom dresses. Glob on the blue eye shadow and mascara that will run when you watch your secret crush slow-dance with another girl. Stuff your bra with Charmin to improve your chances of getting squeezed. Wrist corsage!

the crowd. You know it's time to throw a party when you refer to "hanging out

Boys wear pastel rented tuxedos or pastel shirts with a ruffled front and huge bow tie. Feathered hair parted in the middle, a no-styled mop, or a jumbo Afro. Load up your pockets with breath spray, condoms, a joint, and a flask "borrowed" from someone's dad.

Special Touches:
* Rent a white limo to increase your chances of being voted prom queen.
* Smoking in the bathroom only, in groups of three.
* Jealous fits of tears and broken-hearted misunderstandings are highly encouraged.

Party Games: *Slow-Dancing Make-Out Marathon!* Write every girl's name on a piece of paper and drop in a hat. Each guy picks a girl's name and escorts her onto the dance floor. Pop in a great mix of slow-dancing tunes, turn the lights down low, and signal the start of the make-out marathon. The couple standing and making out the longest wins the right to split up and steal someone else's date. Then the game starts over again!

Party Favor: Unflattering, embarrassing prom photo (Any cute photos must be redone.)

with" TV characters. You know it's time to leave a party when you are standing on

The Trail Mix

Songs with not-so-deep subliminal messages to get your guests to hit the trail:

Walkin' After Midnight *(Patsy Cline)*

Goodbye, Earl *(Dixie Chicks)*

Bye Bye *(Jo Dee Messina)*

Lesson In Leavin'
(Dottie West or Jo Dee Messina)

You Light Up My Life *(Debby Boone)*

Little Goodbyes *(SheDaisy)*

Go Your Own Way *(Fleetwood Mac)*

It's Too Late *(Carole King)*

Send In the Clowns *(A Little Night Music)*

Hit the Road Jack *(Ray Charles)*

Let's Go *(Cars)*

Goodbye Stranger *(Supertramp)*

Uninvited *(Alanis Morissette)*

Leave Me Alone *(Natalie Imbruglia)*

Sleep *(Imogen Heap)*

Bad Girl Wedding Showers

A genuine bad girl is never afraid of the truth. In fact, she loves to find humor in it, build a party around it, and celebrate it with style! If you're looking for tips on traditional wedding showers, keep looking. But if you're looking for tips on prewedding reality, keep reading.

The Cold Shower

Who it's for: Your bride-aholic friend who calls to announce that her (loser, freak, jerky, evil, swishy) boyfriend has popped the question—she's engaged! She's so desperate to be married that she can't see she has a huge problem.

What you do: Do not feign excitement and joy because you think that's what a true friend is supposed to do. Invite only your innermost circle of trusted bad-girl friends. Do not include the Mother of the Bride-aholic, unless she's in your camp. (If this is the case, then let her co-host and pick up the tab. She'll be thrilled.) Remember: A cold shower isn't supposed feel good—it's supposed to wake you up and slap some sense into you! Try these techniques to serve up a healthy dose of relationship reality.

Anonymous Truth (AT). Ask each bad-girl friend to write up an AT about the ill-fated marriage-to-be. This could be an open, honest statement about her fiance:

"Stan is a sorry excuse for a man. He's rude, inappropriate, he treats you like crap, and hits on me after two drinks."

a table screaming "I'm the king of the world!" You know it's time to throw a party

An AT can also be an open, honest statement about your friend's behavior since she met her fiance:

"Ever since you started dating Nick, you have lost your independence, your spine, your personality, and, frankly, my respect."

Assign a bad-girl friend to pack a bag for the bride-aholic. This should contain toiletries, condoms, panty-liners, a change of sexy clothes, a sassy pair of mules.

Order a small bouquet of flowers and follow these steps exactly:

LURE Under the guise of an early wedding shower, lure the bride-aholic to a neutral, safe apartment or house.

LUBRICATE Get the drinks flowing immediately. Remember, alcohol = truth serum (and painkiller).

COMMUNICATE This is the moment of truth. All bad girls join hands and form a loving circle around the bride-aholic. At first she will think this is a fun, silly game some zany friend cooked up. Let her think that. Then the hostess steps up and initiates the intervention with an honest, caring statement filled with love:

"We all love you and care about your future and honestly believe that if you marry _____, you will regret it for the rest of your life."

Then the hostess hands the bride-aholic her bouquet, with all the folded ATs tucked in between the flowers.

ERADICATE The bride-aholic must read each AT aloud. If she's too emotional or violent to read, then other

when you've already heard all the gossip in the latest *People* magazine. You know bad-girl friends can read them aloud, until all the ATs have been expressed.

CELEBRATE After the bride-aholic breaks down and admits that you are all right and Stan is all wrong, it's time to celebrate. After all, now she's single!

EVACUATE That weekend bag was packed with healing in mind:

Take your bad girl party on the road and for a wild weekend (see *The Bad Girl's Guide to the Open Road*). When the bride-aholic tosses her bouquet from the speeding car, relationship rehab is just around the bend!

Ms. Baddy Manners says . . . Relax, honey. Breaking off an engagement isn't the end of the world—but marrying the wrong guy sure as hell is! P.S. It's much more fun to be engaging to many than engaged to just one.

Party Prescriptions from *Dr. Bad Girl*

Your symptoms:
You're sick and tired of your same old, safe hair, clothes, and general look but too afraid to break free of your own expectations.

Your bad girl cure:
Throw a Bad Girl Makeover Party!
- Pull out the shampoo, the champagne, the cosmetics drawer, the hot rollers, the curling iron, the home hair-dying kit, and your wildest bad girl dreams.
- Everyone picks a famous bad girl (or style) and charts out her makeover plan.
- Take a sad girl photo, work your makeover magic, then take a bad girl photo.

---

it's time to leave a party when you hope you will run into your dentist. You know

The Single-Power Shower

Who it's for: Any hot, single bad girl! Just because you haven't found a soul mate doesn't mean you don't need new china, a blender, a wok, more All-Clad, a set of wine glasses, a bike rack, and a tent right now! When you're single—and proud of it—and have absolutely no intention of getting married in the near future, throw yourself a Single-Power Shower! Get all the stuff you want and celebrate your single status in self-loving style.

What you do: Invite other single girls and send out pastel-pink construction paper invitations with dried flowers attached.

Front of Card: *"Somebody's Getting Married . . ."*

Inside Card: *"And it sure as hell ain't me!"*

Paste in a photo of you and the current love of your life (e.g., your dog, car, garden, snowboard, most recent wrought-iron sculpture...) with the usual party details and a long list of the places where you're registered.

How to Register. Most stores will ask for the groom's name, so be prepared. Clip this Pocket Groom Name Finder and keep it handy in your purse or wallet. Depending upon your mood, you may want to use a different groom's name at every stop.

Ms. Baddy Manners says . . . Honey, register everywhere! You deserve the best—in every color and size available.

it's time to throw a party when you start every sentence with "I was listening to

Pocket Groom Name Finder

	First Name	Last Name	Examples
Groovy Groom	your favorite form of birth control	your favorite novelist	*Rubber Hemingway* *Rhythm King* *Norplant Woolf*
Exotic Foreign Groom	your favorite motorcycle	your favorite shoe label	*Ducati Camper* *Harley Puma* *Indian Clergerie*
Multi-culti Groom	first name of your favorite male celebrity	last name of the first boy you ever kissed	*Benecio Swimmer* *Russell Epstein* *Denzel McMullen*
Sporty Groom	your dog's name	last name of your favorite male celebrity	*Buster Cruise* *Rex Ledger* *Sparky Hartnett*

The Psycho Shower

Who it's for: Your seemingly normal bad-girl friend who becomes totally psycho a month after her engagement.

What you do: You and her best baddy friends unite to scare her back to reality before it's too late. Ideally, the invitation features the psycho bride-to-be in a frightening moment of control freakiness—looking so scary even she has to laugh. Of course, the gift theme is knives and shower accessories (caddies, curtains, caps, soap on a rope, bath towels). The point is to show her that if she doesn't get a grip, she'll end up crazier than her mother!

The Newly Wedding Planner Game! Each guest is responsible for recalling a particularly ridiculous example of the bride-to-be's post-engagement pyscho behavior. Guests forward these episodes to the hostess, who transforms them into questions for the game.

Questions might be something like . . .

* *How many trees died so that _____'s wedding organizational flowchart could live?*
* *While shopping for bridesmaids' dresses, how many times did _____ sigh and say, "God, I wish all my friends were a perfect size six?"*
* *How many more times a week does _____ see her personal trainer than she sees her best friend?*
* *How often does _____ burst into tears while reading bridal magazines on a typical morning commute?*
* *At how many different online wedding registries has _____ hit "Select All"?*

NPR . . . " You know it's time to leave a party when you light the wrong end of a

The Pyscho Bride is seated on a cushy thronelike chair. One by one, each guest sits next to her on a small wooden stool, and the hostess asks the pair one of the questions. By the end of the game, she'll either be laughing at the absurdity of her recent behavior and getting some perspective—or she'll never speak to you again.

cigarette and don't notice until someone points it out. You know it's time to throw

The Bad Girl Bachelorette Bash

One of your best bad girls is taking the leap, tying the knot, and heading into the great abyss called marriage. It's a bittersweet occasion. You're happy for her but you know that things will never be quite the same. The Bad Girl Bachelorette Bash is a final send-off, a way to celebrate the bad girl bride—your one-and-only singular friend—and, of course, publicly humiliate her and capture it all on film. Use these activities as the foundation for your fun and you'll all find Bachelorette Party nirvana in no time.

Ms. Baddy Manners says . . . Be sure to serve your guests penis straws at the beginning of the evening so they won't spill a drop of cocktail all night long.

The Bad Girl Bride's To-Do List!
Before the night is done, the bride-to-be must . . .

❏ Order a Blow Job shot and drink it without using her hands.

❏ Kiss a bartender on the lips.

❏ With a straight face, order this round: "I'd like a Sex on the Beach, two Slippery Nipples, and four, no make that five, Screaming Orgasms."

❏ Do the Bad Girl dance on the bar (see page 152).

❏ Grab a mike and sing with the band.

❏ Take off her bra without leaving the room.

❏ Grab a cute guy's butt and squeeze hard.

❏ Grab a cute girl's butt and squeeze gently.

❏ Convince a stranger that she is still a virgin.

❏ Ask a cute guy for exact change—and explain it's the amount needed for the condom machine in the ladies room.

a party when all of your wildest stories took place in the eighties. You know it's

Party Game: *Cucumber Carving Contest.* Each bad girl receives a large uncircumcised cucumber and a vegetable peeler. The contestant who carves her cucumber into the most convincing, lifelike penis wins a Blow Job shot on the girls.

Special Touches: *Bad Boy Stripper.* Anyone can hire a professional stripper for a bachelorette party, but it takes a bad girl to persuade (read bribe, beg, or blackmail) a hot and hunky friend of the bride-to-be to show up and take it all off. (Actually, it's not that hard to do, especially if the guy has a body he loves and wants everyone else to love too!)

Single Girl Gift Salute. Guests are invited to give the bride-to-be super-hot gifts to help her remember—and celebrate in marriage—the best parts of being sexy: the *Kama Sutra;* naughty lingerie; a large, hot pink vibrating dildo; and other sex store goodies that might tickle her fancy.

How to Enjoy a Blow Job

* Pour 1 ounce of Amaretto into a shot glass.

* Top with dollop or swirl of whipped cream.

* Lock hands behind back.

* Wrap mouth around glass, throw head back, and swallow!

Bad Girl Vows

Just because you're getting married doesn't mean you can't be a bad girl anymore. Join hands with other bad girls in a circle and proclaim the following:

"I promise to take you, Bad Girls, as my awfully baddest friends. To have and to hold, in badness and in health. I vow not to lose my bad and turn into a boring married person who stays home every night polishing my husband's shoes and the kitchen floor. I promise to uphold the Bad Girl code, spreading good times and the Bad Girl gospel wherever I go. I vow to maintain my Girl's Night In and Girl's Night Out duties, to go out dancing at least once a month, to continue to show off my bootalicious booty, and to always refer to myself as 'I' rather than 'we.' I vow to maintain my bad, from this day forward, 'til death do us party."

When you have completed these vows, you may kiss your bad-girl friends, who then pronounce you Forever Bad.

More Bad Girl Bachelorette Ideas

Over-30 Bachelorette Bash

Blow off the bar scene and hit the spa for a weekend of serious relaxing and bad girl bonding. Once you have exhausted your-self with self-love and heart-to-hearts, you'll be good and ready for a stiff drink. Then take the bride out on the town and see what happens.

Ms. Baddy Manners says . . . Statistics show that mar-ried women attending over-30 bachelorette parties yield the baddest behavior of all. And honey, if you're going to be a statistic—that's the kind to be!

Over-40 Bachelorette Smash

Get the girls together and sit around telling stories about what you used to do when you still had the energy to be bad, while you drink the finest champagne—or sparkling cider. Be sure to play music from the era when you were all at your baddest—and pray for a few good flashbacks!

The Bogus Bachelorette Party

Who needs a real bride when you've got a smooth stretch ride? Just rent a limo, choose a bogus bride (don't forget her veil), and follow the recipe for the clas-sic Bad Girl Bachelorette Bash. You and your bad girl posse get to wow the crowd and mooch free stuff at every stop. Good, clean fun—and nobody gets hurt.

throw a party when you get laid off with a big, fat severance package. You know

The Truth About Men and Shoes

Shoe Style	What He Thinks It Says	What It Really Says
Worn Gucci loafers	I'm old money.	I'm old.
Athletic shoes	I came from the gym.	I work at a gym.
Birkenstocks	I'm socially responsible.	I'm socially retarded.
Expensive Italian loafers	I'm very successful, worldly, and wealthy.	I've never been in a committed relationship, otherwise she would've told me never to wear these again.
Flip flops	I'm totally cool.	I'm a total fool.
Penny loafers	I'm a relaxed classic.	I can't afford those Italian loafers and I have no idea what else to wear.

Square-toed black boots	I've got it going on.	I've got a girlfriend who dresses me—or I'm gay.
Clogs	I'm a sexy chef.	I'm a smelly chef.
Cowboy boots	I'm like the Marlboro man.	I like the Marlboro man.
Skater sneaks	No one tells me how to dress.	No one told me this was a grown-up party.
Wingtips	I'm a serious lawyer or work in upper management.	I need serious style management.
Combat boots	I'm a bad-ass artist, a social rebel, and an anarchist.	I have a bad cockroach problem in my apartment.
Fabulous pumps	I've got great legs.	Oops. Wrong party!

Bad Girl Baby Showers

Bad girls like to keep things different, fresh, and funny—especially when it comes to traditional girl stuff like baby showers. All you have to do is look for the truth and the humor in the situation—and celebrate it by hosting the most appropriate baddy baby shower.

The Rosemary's Baby Shower

Party Predicament: How to celebrate when you know the mother-to-be (MTB) is conflicted about being pregnant. Don't ignore the feelings, help her explore the feelings! If you think she can handle it, use newborn diapers for invitations and write the party details with a juicy brown pen.

Party Favors: Each guest receives a tub of cocoa butter for unsightly stretch marks, a pacifier, and a video of a classic baby horror film. Try *Rosemary's Baby, Alien, The Exorcist,* any Chucky flick, *The Bad Seed.*

Party Games: *Stinky, Drinky Barney Sing-a-Long!* When guests arrive, each gets a pillow to shove up her dress or down her pants, a juice box spiked with vodka, and a doll with a dirty diaper. The hostess puts on a Barney video at top volume and all guests must dance and sing along whether or not they know the words.

Baby Monitor Madness! All guests divide into two teams, except for the MTB. (Get used to it, MTB. You don't get to play anymore, you just do all the work!) While the MTB tries to nap with the baby monitor near her head, guests take turns hiding in different parts of the house with the other baby monitor. After lulling the MTB

116

into a false state of relaxation, the hiding guest bursts into tears, causing the MTB to race around the house desperately trying to find the crying baby. The hostess keeps score with a stopwatch. The team whose players hide from the MTB the longest wins a trip to McDonald's!

Find the Binky, Now! The MTB is sent off to the kitchen to do dishes while all the guests hide their pacifiers around the house. (Favorite hiding places: under the sofa, under the sofa cushions, in the dog's dish, in the toilet.) When all binkies have been hidden, the guests return to the main room and all start to scream and cry at the tops of their lungs. Each guest gets to scream bloody murder (and sip Bloody Marys) until the MTB finds her lost binky, washes it, and returns it to her mouth.

Party Life Force: Realizing there's nothing wrong with your maternal feelings—especially if they don't line up with every PC parenting book—and knowing there are damn good reasons to be terrified by motherhood.

number of their therapist. You know it's time to throw a party when your closet is

The "Baby? What Baby?" Shower

Party Predicament: How to celebrate not conforming to the maternal norm and honor women who don't have a baby—and don't want one.

Party Games: *Stroller Patrol!* Take to the streets, ideally in a neighborhood known for its high stroller per capita ratio. Wrap a watermelon in a blanket and place your little bundle of joy in a baby stroller. Push stroller down crowded sidewalk, careful not to spill your cocktail or drop your cell phone. Stage stroller wipeouts that send your "baby" flying in front of passing motorists and pedestrians.

Top Ten Reasons Not to Pop! You all sit around coming up with the 10 most meaningful reasons not to have a baby now. Such as:

10. my new white sofa
9. Max, cute guy from the gym
8. Max, me, my new white sofa
7. I already have a full-time job I love
6. my incredibly sexy stomach
5. drinking, smoking, and staying up late
4. sleeping all day
3. the half-finished novel in my laptop
2. Italy
1. all of the above

Party Life Force: Knowing you have the smarts, the confidence, and the right not to have a baby unless you want to—even though all of your friends are doing it and every person you've ever met keeps asking you when you're going to have a baby.

organized by color. You know it's time to leave a party when people keep handing

Things to Do with . . . the Passed-Out Person

* Dress up in old bridesmaid dresses for fun after-hours photo shoot, then mail photos to parents, boss, and/or significant other.

* Place on hardwood floor and play spin the passed-out person with other guests.

* Put his or her hand in bowl of warm water to induce junior-high, late-night slumber-party fun.

* Cover with a warm blanket and use for extra bench seating.

* Lift and drop limbs repeatedly to illustrate your intellectual discussion on the laws of gravity.

* Prop up and embrace passionately to induce jealousy in curious ex-boyfriends or to ward off unwanted suitors.

* Use as backrest to watch late-night television.

* Prop up in back seat of car so you can use the carpool lane.

you glasses of water and giving you their hangover tips. You know it's time to

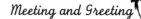

Meeting and Greeting

Ms. Baddy Manners says . . .

* When meeting lots of new people, use a mnemonic device to help remember every name, such as Naughty Nick, Saucy Susan, Lusty Larry, Perverted Pam, Tasty Tom, Moaning Mona, Big Brad, Hot Hank. Repeat each name out loud until memorized.

* If someone mistakes you for someone else, play along and see how far you can take it just for fun!

* When shaking someone's hand, always make eye contact and gently caress your new friend's palm with your ring finger and pinky to set yourself apart from the crowd.

* When meeting a person who goes by two names (Richard/Dick, Andrew/Randy-Andy, Candace/Candy) and you're not sure which name to use, ask this simple question and you'll be in the know from the get go: "Which name do you respond to in bed?"

* Too shy to ask for that adorable someone's name and number? Just collect business cards for the midnight raffle. Get cards from everyone—put the keepers in your right pocket and the losers in your left.

* When a man you're not the least bit interested in asks for your number, gladly give it to him—with two numbers transposed. This technique gets you what you want, and no one gets hurt.

* Can't remember someone's name even though you've met a million times? Just call him "cupcake," "sweet thang," or "honey bun," and he'll never notice.

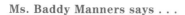

throw a party when your mother starts setting you up with people. You know it's

bad girl mentoring

A true bad girl doesn't hoard all the fun to herself—she shares it with others. With a little effort, you can reach out to good girls in need and help them explore and accept their higher bad girl power. When you spread the bad girl gospel, you'll be riding the express elevator to God's penthouse—and she throws a killer party.

Mother and Wild Child Reunion

Maybe you're one of the lucky ones, a girl with a fun, happy, confident mother who's loving life and in touch with her bad girl self. Maybe, but probably not. If you really love your mother, you'll reach out and help her before it's too late.

Her invitation to the bad girl party life must be subtle or else you'll scare her off. Read a *Bad Girl's Guide* in front of her, and laugh wildly. When she asks what you're reading, tell her it's not for her, she just wouldn't understand. Then put it down and forbid her to read it. When you catch her reading it later, pretend to throw a fit and hide it where you know she'll find it. When your mom starts writing her to-do list on a pantyliner, you know it's time for the Mother and Wild Child Reunion! You and your bad girl posse invite your mothers to join you for an evening of bad girl bonding. You may be surprised by how much bad girl ground you share between you. Amazingly enough, when your Mom is having a lot of fun, she can actually be a lot of fun—who knew?

And don't forget bad girl grannies. All your granny may need is an invitation to cut loose.

time to leave a party when the chandelier looks like it could hold you. You know

Bad Girls in Training

Remember your first training bra? A BGIT Bash serves a similar party life purpose. It helps girls to develop in a safe, supportive environment and makes them feel a part of grown-up things—without attracting too much attention. Keep in mind that the good girl you save could become your best bad-girl friend.

The Pig-Out Party

It's the mother of all BGIT bashes! Encourage girls to celebrate their age, their appetite, and their fast, furious metabolisms with an annual Pig-Out Party—because every young BGIT body is beautiful no matter its shape or size! Eat like a pig with all of your friends and be proud. A genuine bad girl knows that her body is always beautiful and always worth celebrating—just because it's hers. Remember: no dieters, no shame, no guilt, no regrets, and no barfing allowed!

Invitations: Crumpled candy wrappers with party details written on the back with fruity and candy-scented markers. Seal each envelope with a scratch-and-sniff food sticker. Request that each guest bring her favorite snack.

Attire: Comfy, elastic-waist pants and a belly-baring shirt.

Decor: Before guests arrive, set up various pig-out stations throughout the house—a "platter of plenty" on the kitchen table with samples of each treat to come. Have plenty of bowls, plates, utensils, and napkins on hand.

Set up a Digestion Den in the TV room with a Food Coma Couch and other comfortable lounging spots where guests can relax after pig-out sessions.

Menu: The question is not "What's on the menu?," it's "What's not on the menu?" Anything and everything you and your baddies love to eat should be available—no holds barred. Be sure to cover all of the categories in the Junk Food Pyramid—hot, salty, crunchy, sweet, sticky, cold, creamy, and doughy. Be innovative when mixing dishes. Who says Doritos and Oreos don't go together? Break all the rules. Don't hold back—this is a Pig-Out Party. (Special Note: Serve hot ginger tea with lemon between pig-out sessions to aid in digestion and soothe exhausted stomachs.)

Party Game: *The Buddha Belly Contest*
As guests arrive, determine the circumference of each tummy in its "before" state. (Use a tape measure for accuracy.) Record measurements and begin to feast. Once your guests have eaten all they possibly can, each guest gets measured again, then parades around the room, catwalk style, showing off her glorious Buddha Belly. Let it jiggle, let it wiggle! The bad girl whose Buddha belly has grown the most wins everyone's respect and a temporary Buddha tattoo on her tummy!

Party Favors:
* Tums, Alka-Seltzer, and Rolaids
* Minty chewing gum (stimulates digestive acids)
* Bag balm (a rich salve originally designed to soothe cows' udders) to rub on distended tummies

Arty-Farty Party

Host a fabulous evening (or afternoon) of creative bliss. Stock up on glue, glitter, beads, gel pens, wire, tooth-picks, marshmallows, magazines, nuts, bolts, and anything else you can scrounge up, then invite all your creative genius BGITs over. Have a designer pantyliner con-test to see who can turn her pantyliner into the most fabulous work of art. Transform tampons into groovy, glittering jewelry.

(They can wear them to school and see if anyone notices!) Make a bad girl altered-ego collage that reflects their developing bad girl selves. Have them build a shrine to their favorite bad girl icon. If you think they're ready, help them feel comfortable with condoms by blowing them up and making them into condom balloon ani-mal hats!

You know your party's a success when . . .

You know your party is a success when everyone is dancing to the beat of your smoke alarm.

You know your party is a success when someone snorts a Jell-O shot.

You know your party is a success when your entire collection of expensive wine becomes a collection of inexpensive candleholders.

You know your party is a success when some guy is slow-dancing with your potted palm tree.

You know your party is a success when someone is drinking from your dog's dish.

You know your party is a success when you find a black lace bra in the freezer the next morning.

You know your party is a success when your guests are playing ultimate Frisbee with your CDs.

You know your party is a success when your landlady is dancing with your date.

You know your party is a success when those angry young gang members from the corner are dirty dancing with all your girlfriends from the office.

You know your party is a success when there's a naked couple singing and dancing in your shower.

You know your party is a success when all the food, booze, and silverware are gone.

You know your party is a success when all the boys and girls have swapped clothes.

Overthrowing the Party

The only thing more satisfying than throwing your own party is overthrowing someone else's party! You get to enjoy all the fun without having to lift a finger. All it takes is a little planning, a little confidence, and a lot of bad girl attitude. Just open your baddy bag of tricks, ignite that fun fuse, and you'll get any party popping. When you breathe the Party Life into stuffy soirées, dull dinners, office mixers, or family gatherings, everyone will thank you—especially the host and hostess!

party a go-go
or party a no-no?

Sometimes, a party just isn't happening enough to be in the bad girl swirl. The tunes aren't quite right, the social mix is lumpy, or the vibe is just wrong for your mood. The truth is, you don't have time for that! Every minute of the Party Life is precious and so are you.

When you have any doubts about a party's fun factor, it's time to enlist the Bad Girl Party Patrol—a special unit of clever commandos, highly trained in covert operations, social surveillance, and recreational reconnaissance. Known as the Pink Berets in social circles around the world, they can get in and out of any sucky party in 60 seconds without suffering cocktail weenie breath, the cheap beer blues, or a dull conversation hangover.

With the operations manual that follows, you and your ragtag posse of bad girls can become professional Pink Berets.

127

Party Patrol Operations Manual

Before entering the building…

* Designate a party patrol commander to call the shots.
* Each member of your patrol accepts a specific mission to assess and report back on the quantity and quality of one or more of the following:
  1. the tunes
  2. the booze
  3. the food
  4. the crowd
  5. the men's shoes (see "The Truth About Men and Shoes," page 114)
* Your patrol agrees upon a meeting place and time to reconnoiter (such as the hall closet in 45 seconds, the back porch in 90 seconds).
* Synchronize your watches and your quality standards.

Before entering the party…

Perform an external visual inspection. Climb a trellis or a nearby tree or telephone pole to sneak a peek inside a window. If necessary, be prepared to form a human surveillance pyramid.

Do an audio investigation. Press a glass, a stethoscope, or your ear to the front door and listen for sounds of healthy Party Life.

Perform a quick internal exam. If possible, open the door a crack and make a speedy scan of the room using a

recognize someone you used to baby-sit. You know it's time to throw a party when

compact mirror or a pair of reflective sunglasses. If the scene isn't too scary, then proceed with your mission.

Stagger your entrances by a few seconds, with one or two patrol members walking in backwards to disorient anyone who might be watching. Immediately fan out in different directions and complete your assignments with stealth and style. When your patrol reconvenes, everyone gets one vote—it's the ultimate democratic process. After voting, it's either Party a Go-Go or Party a No-No. In the event of a tie, the patrol member wearing the most fabulous party shoes breaks the tie.

Party Prescriptions from *Dr. Bad Girl*

Your symptoms:
You're angry, hurt, confused, and up for revenge—someone has done you wrong. You know who but you don't know why.

Your bad girl cure:
Throw a Voodoo Party!
- Invite all your guests to make a voodoo doll of your enemy out of old socks, yarn, and buttons.
- Light candles.
- Turn on your favorite CD and poke dolls vigorously to the beat of the music.
- Write your enemy's name nine times on a piece of parchment paper. Then blow your nose into the paper and throw it out with the garbage at dusk.
- Pack up voodoo dolls in a box and mail directly to your enemy with a heartfelt note.

you believe your goldfish can recognize your voice. You know it's time to leave a

How to Crash a Party

Crashing a party is a lot like applying makeup—blend, blend, blend, and then blend some more. Once you've got that straight, then all you need is confidence, a fabulous party outfit, and a great exit strategy, in case of an emergency.

When crashing a party . . .

1. Always bring a gift for the hostess.
2. Find your point man quickly.

To party crash successfully, you always want a point man, a guy whose name you know who you can point at from across the room if someone challenges your reason for being there. As you become more experienced and skilled at party crashing, challenge yourself by crashing smaller and smaller gatherings. When you're really good, you'll be crashing dinner parties for eight!

Last-Minute Hostess Gifts

* nicely wrapped video you don't ever watch
* potted plant from her front doorstep
* fresh cut flowers from her garden
* two rolls of toilet paper in a handsome gift bag
* this book

party when you recognize someone who used to baby-sit you. You know it's time

Reasons to Crash a Party

* nothing good on TV tonight

* adventure

* good clean fun

* great opportunity to use a new alias

* promotes team building among your personal posse

* free food and drinks

* new material for your memoirs

* instantly expand your social circle

* the thrill of the chase—out the front door and down the steps

* the movie was sold out

* personal challenge that's safer than rock climbing

* get decorating ideas without paying decorator prices

* your dating pool is shallow and drying up

* meet exciting new people you'll never have to see again if you do something really crazy

* the night is still young and so are you

* bad girl duty (the host will thank you later!)

* more fun than crashing a car

Making Introductions

Ms. Baddy Manners says . . .

* Intercept all casual air kisses with soft, open loving lips. (Jump-start new relationships and old relatives' pacemakers, too!)

* Say "eat" when you mean to say "meet" and see if anyone notices.

    "Hello, I've been dying to eat you all night!"

    "So nice to eat you, Rabbi Lehman."

    "Susan, this way. You simply must eat Robert!"

* When introducing people for the first time, it's always helpful to mention a spicy personal detail or topic of common interest to help ignite their conversation.

    "Jill meet Page. She dyes her hair, too!"

    "Nick, this is Samantha. She was arrested for indecent exposure just last month!"

    "Marlena, meet Brett. He can't stay awake at the office either!"

    "Paul, this is my dear friend Maggie. She's in denial about her sexuality just like you!"

    "Roger, you must know Eduardo. You have so much in common—like Gina! You were both dating her all fall."

    "Cathy, let me introduce Carl. He can't hold his liquor either!"

    "Ricky, let me introduce Sheila. She loves mountain biking and cyber porn almost as much as you do!"

to throw a party when you accidentally kiss your pet on the lips and feel a tingle.

Making an Entrance

Any bad girl worth her leopard-print party panties knows the importance of first impressions—and knows how to turn heads in a crowded room. When she arrives at a party, she makes an entrance with bad girl style—or else she doesn't bother to go at all.

When flying solo . . .

* Spill your change purse in the foyer, cueing everyone to catch a titillating glimpse of your cleavage when you bend over.
* Catch your dress in the door and keep on walking, until you've ripped yourself a new mini skirt.
* Wear a miner's headlamp and check everyone's ID.
* Climb in a window from the fire escape carrying a cat.
* Slide across the hardwood floor on your knees like a rock star.
* Jump out of a cake.
* Wear a scarf and large, dark glasses and whisper frantically into a cell phone as you enter, looking around the party suspiciously.
* Wear a trench coat and when you walk in, flash the party a big smile and everything else you've got.
* March in twirling a flaming baton, singing "God Bless America."

You know it's time to leave a party when eating the worm seems like a good idea.

When partying with your personal posse . . .

Charlie's Angels Entrance

Perfect for threesomes when you and your gal pals just happen to be sporting water pistols, big pink shades, tiny T's, and tight bell bottoms.

Kick open the door, dash in like you're in hot pursuit, then strike a sexy pose until all heads are turned and all the men are at your mercy.

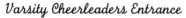

Varsity Cheerleaders Entrance

Perfect for large groups of girls with small pleated skirts and a secret desire to show off their legs, undies, and everything else.

Prance into the room in single file, then fall into formation and do your best/worst cheerleading moves (high kicks are a must) until the crowd is on its feet cheering for your team.

All-Girl Band Entrance

Perfect for party crashing when you're dressed way too groovy for the scene and just happen to be sporting soft guitar cases, shades, super-tight tank tops with tough-girl leather, and attitude. (The host will be too intimidated by your cool to challenge you.)

Strut into the room with your shades on. Say, "Have you seen our publicist? She said this was going to be a kick-ass party," while flicking your cigarette ash into someone's cocktail glass. Then add, "Be cool, okay? No autographs tonight."

You know it's time to throw a party when your anal roommate leaves town. You

Super Bad Girl to the Rescue!

Often a busy hostess doesn't have time for all the last-minute finishing touches to make her party a success. Fortunately, a super bad girl comes to a party prepared to give the harried hostess the support she needs and deserves—to transform a snoozy party into a doozy of a rager! If things feel stuffy, stale, or sucky, just pull one of these tricks out of your baddy bag and watch the party come to life!

Spike it!

* **Spike the Punch:** What a bummer, the hostess didn't have time to buy that extra gallon of vodka for the punch. What a stealth bomber, you did!

* **Spike the Music:** Unfortunately, the hostess wasn't able to find any of her decent CDs. Fortunately, you burned and packed a special party mix just for this occasion!

* **Spike the Buffet:** Sadly, the hostess forgot to add the best little treats to her buffet table. Happily, you've got a party platter of condoms, pop rocks, and scintillating, suggestive fortune cookies in your shoulder bag!

* **Spike the Jerk:** Oh no, the hostess forgot to un-invite that drunken dancing fool who steps on everyone's toes. Oh yeah, just slip on your killer spiked heels and stomp backward till he hops and drops!

Stir the Social Mix

Stupid Cupid. This game is fun to play alone or with friends! With all the sincerity you can muster, randomly approach strangers and whisper one of these lines:

know it's time to leave a party when you've been waiting for 10 minutes to get

"He likes you, he really likes you. But he's so shy."

"She's so into you. Go say hello before she leaves."

"This is going to sound crazy, but that beautiful blonde over there wants your number."

"That cutie is dying to dance with you. Go for it!"

Keep working the crowd until you've got the whole party whipped into a frothy, tangled love swirl. If anyone challenges you, just say, "Whoops! I thought you were someone else."

Spitball Blowout. If you thought launching spitballs was fun in junior high, wait until you play it now! The stakes are even higher now and the targets are much more interesting than Mrs. Olsen's bouffant.

What you need:

* other bored party guests with strong salivary glands
* cocktail napkins, straws, Bic pens
* impeccable aim

What you do:

Tear off small piece of cocktail napkin, discreetly slip into mouth for appropriate saliva coat, take aim, and spit hard. Use the following point system to determine a winner:

spitball in punch bowl	5 points
spitball in busty guest's cleavage	8 points
spitball at cute guy's buns	9 points
spitball lodged in over-sprayed 'do	10 points
spitball in loudmouth's open mouth	14 points
spitball in ex's eye	16 points
spitball in ex's new girlfriend's drink	20 points

into a locked closet. You know it's time to throw a party when you hit on tele-

Formal Faux Fart-Off. The perfect game for unstuffing dress-up affairs! Just sneak up behind a guest who's taking him or herself a bit too seriously, and let it rip. When the guest turns around, nod and smile elegantly. When they turn away, do it again!

What you need:
* sleeveless gowns or tops with easy armpit access
* a few fun-lovin' fools to join you

What you do:
Cup one hand firmly in your armpit and flap your arm like a chicken until you achieve a resonant farting sound.

If you're feeling really ambitious, try a knee fart! Simply cup one hand over the back of your knee and kick out your leg like a Rockette. To really get a crowd moving, assemble a kick-line of bad girls and do knee farts in unison!

Ouija Booger! Yes, you and your friends can move the invisible booger across your enemy's face! All you have to do is harness your collective psychic energy.

What you need:
* deserving evil target
* a few willing accomplices in your conversation bouquet

What you do:
Very casually wipe at an imaginary booger on your face until your evil target starts to wipe his/her face like a paranoid fool.

Then give it a rest. When your evil target has temporarily regained his/her composure, an accomplice then subtly wipes at a different spot.

137

The object of the game:

See how long you can keep your victim unconsciously pushing the Ouija booger around.

Bad Girl's Grope. When you don't know anyone (or hardly anyone) at the party, just pretend to be blind! It's the perfect way to grope other guests without getting into trouble or having to pretending to care about mind-numbingly dull conversation.

What you need:

* ability to focus your eyes a foot to the left or right of the person you're talking to
* nerves of steel
* an innocent face

What you do:

Stick with the blind act no matter what. If you bluff well, eventually you'll win over even the skeptics. Introduce yourself to everyone, try to mix your own cocktails, work the crowd, network, flirt, dance. Do everything you would normally do at a party except make eye contact!

Add to the personal challenge by groping for big points! Keep score, then challenge yourself and your friends to top your personal best!

stock market. You know it's time to throw a party when you knit a Christmas

guest wearing leather pants	5 points
guest wearing corduroys	10 points
guest with a bald head	15 points
guest with D cups	20 points
guest with a hairy chest	25 points
guest with a big belt buckle	30 points
guest wearing boxers	35 points
guest wearing briefs	40 points
guest wearing a thong	50 points
guest going commando	100 points

Ms. Baddy Manners says . . . When playing Bad Girl's Grope, be sure to pee in the dark. If you turn on the bathroom light, you're sure to be busted! Trust me.

Mobile Mullet Station. Spice up the party and ignite an '80s revival trend all at once!

What you need:
* hedge trimmers, pinking shears, electric razor
* drunken guests with lots of hair to work with
* sturdy chair or kitchen stool

What you do:
Get some hype going early on in the night about how retro-cool the mullet is.

Set up a Mobile Mullet Station in the kitchen and charge guests three dollars to transform their boring, run-of-the-mill mane into a classic mullet!

Spank Tank. Meet, greet, feel the heat!

What you need:
* wide array of spanking tools (hairbrush, spatula, flyswatter, pasta server, etc.)
* willing participants

tree sweater. You know it's time to leave a party when you start pitching your

Things to Do with . . . The Host's Phone

* Crank call your ex, your boss, and your ex-boss to foil their *69 attempts to bust you.

* Call a 1-900 psychic hotline to get your 12-month personal forecast.

* Give host's number out in advance and receive urgent calls all night to enhance your party popularity.

* Check your messages.

* Check the host's messages.

* Call parents to reveal that you're gay/pregnant/unemployed/ Republican/all of the above, then return to party and drink heavily.

* Check in with old, dear friends across the nation.

* Secretly dial your friend and request a "personal emergency" call for a foolproof excuse to bolt from a dull dinner party.

* Call a cab when you can't find your car keys—or your car.

* If you're not getting any action, call a hot 1-900 number for personal pleasures and tell your friends you need some "me time."

* Call your own voicemail and hold receiver up to record friends' and lovers' late-night drunken promises.

screenplay concept. You know it's time to throw a party when you find the suede

What you do:

Turn a shower stall or closet into a Spank Tank.

Go through the crowd nabbing very hot guests who you suspect have been very bad.

Very bad guests must close their eyes and point to a spanking utensil, then step inside the tank, stick their butts outside, and get what they deserve.

Ms. Baddy Manners says . . . Always be on the lookout for bad guests who may be vulnerable to Fanatical Addiction to Ass Spanking Syndrome (FATASS) and provide ample supervision to avoid spank-tank abuse.

More Ways to Spike the Party

* Seductively French kiss your glass and slowly sip your wine like a cat.
* Whip out a lollipop and know how to use it. (You'll be surrounded by drooling suckers in a flash!)
* When you must wear stockings or pantyhose to a social gathering, cut out the cotton crotch before you go. You'll be feeling free and breezy no matter how stuffy the crowd gets. Saves time when peeing too!
* Streak!
* Slip ice cubes down the back and front of guests' shirts and pants.
* Blow up colored condoms and tape them around the room like balloons.
* Locate the master fuse box and cut off electricity.
* Put finger condoms on cocktail weenies and baby carrots.

boots in your size, on sale. You know it's time to leave a party when even you don't

★ Call and order 12 pizzas with everything. When the doorbell rings, duck into the bathroom until the coast and tab are clear.

★ Whip out two tins of breath mints and shake them like mini maracas until you've got the crowd feeling a loving Latin beat.

★ Go from one conversational cluster to the next asking, "Has anyone seen the rat?"

★ Locate the host's camera and organize an X-rated photo shoot in high-profile locations around the house, starting with the host's bedroom—extra points for guys posing in lingerie!

★ Organize a game of *Blow and Tell.* Gather guests in a circle and let each one tell their naughtiest story of oral triumph with a visual demonstration (works best in intimate, somewhat incestuous groups of friends).

★ Bring a bunch of helium-filled balloons as a hostess gift and when things get dull, start popping and sucking. Once you've achieved a squeaky-high helium voice, try one or all of the following:

  • Grab a microphone (beer bottle, flashlight, or spatula will do) and belt out your favorite tune.

  • Approach a hottie and whisper in his ear, "You Mickey. Me Minnie."

  • Find a phone, dial your boss's number, and leave a psychotic message.

★ Set up a Penny-a-Pierce Stand in the pantry. All you need is ice, rubbing alcohol, and a sharp pin. Offer clients a swig of Jim Beam or Jack Daniels to dull the sensation and poke a hole in ear lobe, bellybutton lobe, nipple, or wherever they so desire.

get the point you're trying to make. You know it's time to throw a party when only

* Hit the pantry, find a roll of tinfoil, and line 'em up for funky face and body molds. Just pull out a sheet of foil and mold it to a guest's face or other feature. Pull away slowly, being careful not to lose the shape. Then other guests try to match the body part to the body!

* Organize the *First Annual Balance the Potted Plant on Your Head Relay Race.* Split willing guests into two relay teams, map out an obstacle course from, say, the bar to the snack table to the dance floor to the rest room to the roof deck then back, and send the contestants running. The first team to finish the course wins their very own potted plant! (Don't mention this part to the host.)

your gynecologist has seen your daring Brazilian bikini wax. You know it's time to

Bad Girl Party Toasts

Just raise your glass and add a touch of bad girl class to any gathering.

The occasion:

For nights when single status seems to sour and your bad girls need to regain their perspective and their auto-erotic power.

The toast:

Here's to the men that we love,
Here's to the men that love us.
But the men that we love,
Aren't the men that love us,
So screw the damn men—here's to us!

The occasion:

Use Dorothy Parker's legendary quotation to summon the bad girl spirit any time you're out drinking martinis with the girls.

The toast:

I like to have a martini,
Two at the very most.
After three I'm under the table,
After four I'm under my host!

(After everyone drinks, smile coyly and whisper, "Dorothy Parker.")

The occasion:

When a group of tired bad girls is slumped around your living room sipping wine and you need to lift their spirits and get them to join the party.

The toast:

Calling all bad girls, it's time for a toast
Here's a message from your foxy host.
Please pour yourself a drink and raise your glass,
Then get up and dance and get off your lazy ass!

The occasion:

When a good girl's success has your bad girl posse wondering if they should switch sides.

The toast:

Here's to the bad girls around the room,
Bad from the moment they left the womb.
May they stay bad for the rest of their days
And always celebrate in racy, ridiculous ways!

The occasion:

One of your baddies has been extra bad and you want to congratulate her.

The toast:

There once was a very bad girl,
With a swirl in the middle of her forehead.
When she was good, she was very, very good.
But when she was bad, she was better!

When Buzz Kills Miraculously

Buzz Kill Having nothing to say all night.
Buzz Thrill Being told you're incredibly mysterious.

Buzz Kill Drinking so much that you jabber on about your
personal problems all night long to strangers.
Buzz Thrill Waking up the next morning feeling healed.

Buzz Kill A hottie passes on you.
Buzz Thrill A hottie passes out on you.

Buzz Kill Arriving late and finding all the shrimp cocktail
has already been eaten.
Buzz Thrill Being the only guest who doesn't end up in the
emergency room with food poisoning.

Buzz Kill Hanging out with a bunch of duds all night.
Buzz Thrill Being the most fascinating person at the party.

Buzz Kill The cops arrive.
Buzz Thrill They turn out to be rent-a-cop strippers.

Buzz Kill Passing out in the hostess's closet.
Buzz Thrill Waking up at home the next morning wearing
new Prada shoes.

Become Buzz Thrills

Buzz Kill Someone introduces you by the wrong name.
Buzz Thrill Someone introduces you by the wrong name to a hunk you had a one-night stand with a year ago.

Buzz Kill Puking in the host's bathroom all night.
Buzz Thrill Waking up five pounds lighter.

Buzz Kill You're stuck in a long conversation with a gynecologist.
Buzz Thrill You're stuck in a locked bathroom with a gynecologist.

Buzz Kill Getting something stuck in your teeth.
Buzz Thrill Having a cute guy offer to get it out with his tongue.

Buzz Kill The cute guy you've been making eyes at kisses his boyfriend.
Buzz Thrill Someone else's boyfriend kisses you.

Buzz Kill Your ride wants to go home early.
Buzz Thrill Your crush wants to take you home late.

Buzz Kill Waking up with a giant hickey.
Buzz Thrill Feeling like a teenager again.

Buzz Kill Seeing your ex show up with a hot babe.
Buzz Thrill Seeing your ex throw up on a hot babe.

Buzz Kill Finding the keg empty.
Buzz Thrill Finding the wine cellar.

Buzz Kill Having the wrong outfit on.
Buzz Thrill Having so much fun you don't even care.

Be a Bad Girl Temp-tress

Looking for exciting, new ways to interact with other party guests? Just choose from one of these tempting temp jobs to get the professional privileges and party perks you deserve. When you do it with confidence and style, everyone qualifies for benefits!

The Temp Job:

Chiropractor

The Perks:

Strangers allow you to run your hands up and down their spines.

Action Plan:

As you're speaking to a handsome stranger, eye his shoulders suspiciously, look him in the eye, and say, "I couldn't help but notice that you're completely out of alignment. May I?"

Once you've introduced yourself as a chiropractor, rub your hand up and down his spine, nodding seriously to yourself, saying "Just what I thought."

When he looks at you pleadingly, make him an offer he can't refuse: "I don't usually do this, but if you want to step into a quiet room for a minute I can give you an adjustment that will change your life."

In the host's bedroom, wrap your arms around him from behind, squeeze hard, and lift until you hear a loud cracking sound, a fart, or a moan of ecstasy. Try not to injure yourself—it blows your cover.

leave a party when you are still dancing long after the music has stopped. You

The Temp Job:
Casting Agent

The Perks:
* Everyone scrambles to impress you with their charm, wit, and good looks.
* You go home with pockets full of cutie head shots—and phone numbers and vital stats—for your personal party Rolodex.

Action Plan:

Wear a Polaroid camera around your neck and carry a small pad of paper and a pen. Look all business.

Walk through the crowd looking people up and down, jotting things down on your notepad.

Get a buzz going. Reluctantly, tell one guest why you're there. "I'm casting for the new Jennifer Aniston/Brad Pitt romantic comedy action thriller." Word will travel faster than a cold streaker.

As you are swarmed by starstruck guests, ask them to form a line and wait patiently. Proceed to snap Polaroids, asking each guest to write his/her name, phone number, height, weight, and any "special skills" on the flap. Feel free to brush off anyone you're not attracted to: "Sorry, you're not right for the part."

know it's time to throw a party when you fall madly in love with someone who's

The Temp Job:
Palm Reader

The Perks:
Titillating hand-to-hand contact leading to intense eye contact and deep conversation about the meaning of life.

Action Plan:
Spot an attractive loner type and approach with purpose and an air of mystery.

Whisper confidently, "I'm here to read your palm," and lead him to a quiet corner.

Gently take his hand in yours and look deep into his eyes as your run your finger down the center of his palm.

Once you've captured his attention, focus on his palm, looking expertly at the web of lines, oohing and ahhing, until you feel his pulse quicken. Then mention that you have other talents besides reading palms.

The Temp Job:

Phone Sex Operator

The Perks:

Getting to talk dirty to hot guests who don't believe you and challenge you to prove it.

Action Plan:

Introduce yourself to a new conversation cluster and act completely normal, participating in the friendly party chatter.

When someone asks what you do, matter-of-factly state, "I work as a phone sex operator while I'm getting my master's."

After the burst of nervous laughter and series of "No way!"s (or dead silence), follow with, "Oh yeah, it's fun and easy. I'll show you."

Select the most attractive guest in the group, direct him to the phone in a bedroom, then pick up the phone in the main room and work your wicked magic. If you can talk the talk, you'll have your pick of the litter.

dance floor. You know it's time to throw a party when you get a great new haircut.

The Bad Girl Dance!

Do it alone, do it with friends, do it with strangers—but definitely do it. The Bad Girl Dance is an open container of self-loving fun and an open invitation to bond with your body and other bad girls. The Bad Girl is the Hustle on ecstasy and the Time Warp on layaway. It's the line dance for girls who like life outside the lines. The Bad Girl will get your juices pumpin' and any party jumpin'. Crank a favorite tune with a strong, steady beat, make some space in the crowd, then start to celebrate the power of one and the power of sexy fun. All steps are on an eight count.

1. Strut forward to the count of four, now back it up and strut some more.

2. Step in place and swing your hips, while you hug yourself and lick your lips.

3. Now swing and step to the left for four, and smack your ass which you adore.

4. Swing and step back to the right, then cup your rack and hold it tight.

5. Air-kiss left, then air-kiss right, and look real sexy 'cause you just might.

6. Do a lovin' thrust as you turn around, then shimmy your booty down to the ground.

7. Shimmy back up and wave to a friend, then step hard right and start again.

Personalize these basic steps with your own kicks, crosses, hops, and grinds and you'll find your own bad girl beat in no time.

A seasoned Party Lifer always comes to the aid of a friend in need, whether she's getting down with a trail of TP on the dance floor or she's unwittingly flashing her nipple in a heated conversation. When you and your girls cover each other with the secret code, you'll get the message across without spilling the beans or killing the mood. It's a group party-life insurance policy—and it's free!

Mid Party Life Crisis	Party Life Saver Code
Her ex boyfriend just walked in.	"The beagle has landed."
Her serious pantyline problem.	"Love the liner notes on your B side!"
Her fly is down.	"Did someone just go riding? The barn door is open."
Toilet paper is stuck to her shoe.	"I watched *The Paper Chase* in a teepee once."
There's spinach in her teeth.	Casually whistle "I'm Popeye the sailor man."
Her breast is exposed.	"Is it me or is it a bit nippy in here?"
The person she's dissing is quickly approaching.	"Claw-foot tub! Claw-foot tub!"
There's mascara gunk in her right eye.	"Your favorite dwarf is still Sleepy, right?"

Party Life Crisis Code

Mid Party Life Crisis	Party Life Saver Code
Impending strapless dress disaster or serious tube-top slippage	"You're really getting down tonight."
Her hair looks really bizarre.	"You're looking as smart as Einstein!"
You've got to pee and tell her something in the ladies' room.	"We must plan a trip to Niagara Falls very soon."
There's a big booger hanging out of her nose.	"UBS delivery!" (United Booger Service)
She's got a bad wedgie.	"Fire in the hole! Fire in the hole!"
Scary inner lipstick erosion	"I was thinking of applying for clown college. How about you?"
Her date is totally trashed.	"Man overboard!"
A cute guy just entered the room.	"Have you seen the new Babe movie yet?"
Some chick is flirting with her man.	"There's a fly in your honey."
Some chicks are circling your man.	"Who let the dogs out?"
You just overflowed the toilet.	"I've got a new theory on the Watergate scandal. Let's talk and walk!"

Bold Bad Girl Banter

If a dull, generic guy asks you a dull, generic question, don't just smile politely and answer it—banter it! When you fire back something weird, warped, or unexpected, he may be totally clueless. But at least you'll be entertained watching him try to figure you out.

The Question	Your Answer
Hey, what's your sign?	Odd-Size Baggage. What's yours?
Isn't this a fun party?	Not half as fun as the one behind that big one-way mirror!
How old are you?	Over 18 and that's all you really need to know.
What do you do for fun on the weekends?	Well, I really like to drive around and look for cute guys on road bikes with really hard, tight asses and then gently hit their back tire and knock them over so I can introduce myself. What about you?

Have we met?	You betcha, you just don't recognize me with my clothes on.
Who did you vote for in the last election?	I voted for myself, of course. If you don't vote for yourself, then how can you expect others to vote for you?
Do you know CPR?	Yeah, I'm pretty sure I dated him in college.
Where do you work?	I don't. I just don't have time for a job.
Have you been on any trips lately?	Why yes! I just got back from an extended stay at the Easy Girl Spa for unwed mothers.
Can I get you a drink?	I don't know, can you?
How did you get so open and in touch with your emotions?	I did est when I was 12.
Seen any good movies?	Nope. But when I go to a movie, I don't waste a second watching it.
Are you a VP?	Yes. I'm VP of marketing interns.
How do you know the host?	Intimately.

party when you find out your nest egg has been fried. You know it's time to leave

The One-Minute Man Translator

Why waste a lot of party time chatting up a mysterious stranger only to find that he's not what you're looking for? With the right leading question, you'll get an answer that tells you all you really want to know.

What you want to know	What you say	What you hope he says
If he's available	Are you here with your fiancée?	Fiancée? Are you nuts? I don't even have a girlfriend.
If he's well adjusted	How's your mother?	She's fine, thanks. I talked to her last week.
If he's healthy and self-aware	How long have you been in therapy?	Not long enough.
If he's gainfully employed	Oh my Gawd, did you see that outrageous Oprah last week?	Nope.
If he's secretly gay	Didn't you just love *Yentl?*	Who?
If he's got a drinking problem	Are you this much fun when you're sober?	I'm a lot more fun.
If he likes bad girls	Want to go for a ride on my motorcycle?	Yeah. Can I drive?

just add bad

Once you've learned how to add bad to a party, you'll never again suffer through a miserable family gathering, stuffy wedding, or boring holiday fest. How do you know it's time to add a little bad? Maybe you're feeling bored, maybe you're feeling ignored, maybe you're feeling mischievous, or maybe you're just being you. Whatever your cause for celebration, just add bad and the fun will follow!

How to Add Bad to . . . Family Gatherings

Play *Bad Family Feud!*
Instead of avoiding conflict at your next family gathering, celebrate it with a fun game of *Bad Family Feud!* Same old rules apply, only this time—it's personal.

What you need:
* two teams, each composed of five members from the same family
* a gregarious (and preferably tipsy) emcee
* video camera on a tripod
* two waist-high nephews or nieces whose small, round heads will serve as makeshift buzzers. (The first yelp of pain signals an answer.)

What you do:
Before the game, secretly poll every player with a question like "Name a relative with a hairpiece" or "Name a relative with really bad credit." Then tally up the top three or four vote getters. (The name with the most votes goes

to the top of the board; the other two or three vote getters follow in order.)

The emcee introduces each family member with a funny little anecdote, then looks into the camera and gleefully cries, "Let's start the Bad Family Feud!"

Two players, one from each team, step forward to face off and answer the secretly surveyed question (example: Name a relative with a hairpiece).

The first player to slap the top of a niece or nephew's head and elicit a yelp gets the first shot at answering the question. Then the other player gets to answer. The player who guesses the top vote getter from the pregame survey wins control of the board and the chance play with his or her team. If the team playing the board gets three wrong answers, they lose control of the board. Following are some sample questions and answers to get things rolling:

and you're talking to the same people. You know it's time to throw a party when

Party Activities

Ms. Baddy Manners says . . .

* When the hors d'oeuvres tray is down to the last two or three pieces, take them all and eat them. Your kindness saves other guests from the pain of having to take the last hors d'oeuvres.

* Never mix cocktails at a party. Always get someone else to mix them for you!

* Should you happen to catch the hostess in a compromising position, always offer a helping hand.

* Going through other guests' coat pockets—party a no-no. Slipping your number into other guests' coat pockets—party a go-go!

* When opening a bottle of champagne, be sure to hold the bottle at a slight angle, aim the cork at a chandelier, and lap up any spillage with your tongue.

* Having sex in the bathroom while guests are waiting to pee—party a no-no. Having sex in the shower while guests are peeing—party a go-go!

your ex-boyfriend invites you to his bachelor party. You know it's time to leave a

Question: Why Mom and Dad sleep in separate rooms?

Survey Says:

* Dad snores!
* Dad's an alcoholic!
* Dad's got really bad gas!

And the number one answer is . . . Mom can't stand sex anymore!

Question: Why our family is flat broke?

Survey Says:

* Mom maxed out the credit cards redecorating the house!
* [Insert sibling's name here] visited that posh rehab center which cost more than four years of college!
* Dad's having a midlife crisis and just bought a Porsche!

And the number one answer is . . . The veterinary and massage bills for Mom's Shih Tzu, Bubbles!

Question: What things [insert your name here] did in high school that Mom and Dad still don't know about?

Survey Says:

* Spent a week in Maui with her tennis instructor instead of going to tennis camp!
* Took the family car to Vegas instead of visiting East Coast colleges!
* Did it in Mom and Dad's bed with young, sexy Father O'Malley.

And the number one answer is . . . Played wide receiver on the varsity football team!

party when you're walking around singing into a pool cue. You know it's time to

Question: Which member of our family has the biggest substance abuse problem?

Survey Says:

* [Insert sibling's name] and his weed
* Dad and his Cuban cigars
* Mom and her Percodan and [Insert sibling's name]'s weed

And the number one answer is . . . Grandma and her bourbon!

More Creative Ways to Add Bad

* Play *Who's That Relative?* Kids get up and do dead-on imitations of their relatives dancing, making toasts, eating, arguing, etc. Other relatives try to guess who they're imitating.
* Gather all the "kids" in the kitchen, and collect all pots, pans, Tupperware, and large wooden spoons. Then form a drumming circle on the floor and lead them in therapeutic celebrations of joy, frustration, rage, and sisterhood.
* Play *Pin the Blame on the Mommy!* Each person in the room explains their psychological, physical, and professional shortcomings and why it's all their mother's fault.
* When your grandfather gets up to make a toast, slip a whoopee cushion onto his chair.
* Pour out all vodka, refill bottles with water, and see how long it takes Auntie Maureen to realize she's not catching a buzz.

throw a party when the last time you "did the salsa" was late last night in front of

How to Add Bad to . . . Weddings

Play *Toasted Toast-Mistress!*

Tap your champagne glass and give an impromptu (scandalous) toast honoring the way the bride actually made out with the stripper at her bachelorette party. Or try one of these Add-Bad classic toasts:

Here's to the handsome groom and his lovely, bad girl bride,
Better fasten the bed sheets, baby, it's gonna be a bumpy ride!

Here's to the lucky bride who loves her handsome groom
Almost as much as the other men standing around the room!

Here's to the lucky groom and his lovely bad girl lass,
He'd better stay in line or she'll kick his sorry ass!

More Creative Ways to Add Bad

* Dirty dance with the priest or clergyman who performed the ceremony.
* Host a silent auction featuring scandalous photos of the bride at her bachelorette party.
* Spread a rumor about the groom to the bride's great-aunt and see how long it takes to get to the bride's mother.

the refrigerator with a bag of stale chips. You know it's time to leave a party when

* Get the catering staff stoned.
* Persuade the flower girls to take off their tights and wear them around their necks like feather boas.

Ms. Baddy Manners says . . . If you can't afford an expensive wedding gift, simply buy an expensive card. Find a large, lavishly wrapped gift then remove the card, replace it with yours, and slip the other card beneath the pile of gifts!

Party Prescriptions from

Dr. Bad Girl

Your symptoms:
You're overwhelmed and depressed. You have so many old clothes you never wear that you can't get the clothes you do wear into your closet.

Your Bad Girl cure:
Throw a Purge Party!
• Invite your guests to tie you to a chair, gag you, then rip through your closets and drawers, mercilessly purging your prehistoric purchases and fashion disasters.
• Extra points are given for items with school insignias, price tags still attached, and pleats.
• Your crop of old clothes goes directly to a local women's shelter, then your gag is removed.

you want to turn on CNN. You know it's time to throw a party when you buy a new

How to Add Bad to . . .
Office Parties

Play *Who Moved All the Cheese?*

What you need:

* typical corporate office building
* typical corporate party cheese tray stacked a mile high
  with cheese cubes that no one will ever eat
* nothing to lose

What you do:

Collect a few disgruntled co-workers.

Collect cheese cubes by the handful and stash them in your pockets or plastic cups.

Nonchalantly wander around the party. When no one is looking, take aim and all try to toss your cheese into the overhead lighting. At the next Monday morning status meeting, you'll have stinky fondue!

Make melted cheese paper sandwiches on the copier.

Slip off to your boss's office and replace all the keys on her computer keyboard with cheese cubes.

Stash the remaining cubes in bookcases, in the back of the office bitch's desk drawers, and anywhere else you want to add lasting bad.

outfit for your niece's second birthday party. You know it's time to leave a party

You know your party was a success when . . .

You know your party was a success when you get your film developed and don't recognize one person on the roll.

You know your party was a success when you find a guy sound asleep on your sofa wearing your old Girl Scout uniform.

You know your party was a success when the Chinese food leftovers from six weeks ago are gone from the back of the fridge.

You know your party was a success when you find the pizza delivery guy in bed with your roommate.

You know your party was a success when you wake up and find dollar bills in your underwear.

You know your party was a success when the rug is rolled up in the corner and there's a pair of feet sticking out the end.

You know your party was a success when you wake up in a place you don't recognize and it's your living room.

You know your party was a success when you read about it in the paper.

You know your party was a success when your friend calls to thank you for the great advice you gave her last night and you have to ask her what you said.

You know your party was a success when it's still going as you head out the door to work.

You know your party was a success when a group of strangers shows up at your door the next night asking when the rave starts.

More Creative Ways to Add Bad

* Slip into the ladies' room and, when you know the stalls are loaded, tell your friend in stage whispers about the CEO's secret life as an exotic dancer.
* Call in a bong threat: "There's a bong in the building. I repeat, a bong in the building."
* Point out office brown-nosers by directing a red laser pointer up their nostrils from across the room.
* Carry a porn flick in your purse and, when nobody's looking, slip it in with the tapes for a new advertising campaign.

Party Prescriptions from

Dr. Bad Girl

Your symptoms:
You're bloated, pimply, crampy, crabby, and weepy.

Your bad girl cure:
Throw a PMS Party!
* Take two chocolate bars every four hours.
* Bitch and snap at all guests. (They, of course, should be bitchy and snappy too!)
* Relax with sappy rented movie, bawling as needed.
* Repeatedly rinse back of throat with Scotch or brandy.

when the karaoke machine comes out—and you won't give anyone else a turn.

Things to Do in . . . a Locked Bathroom

* Create detailed personality profile of host based on contents of medicine chest.

* Assess prescription stock for drug problems or party opportunities.

* Hold private counseling session for troubled guests.

* Give free mini-facials and touch-ups to all female party guests.

* Stock up on essentials like tampons, dental floss, and pantyliners.

* Fill the tub with fresh towels, draw the shower curtain, and take a restorative disco nap.

* Light candles, run a steamy bubble bath, and invite a hot guy to join you.

* Bring in journals lifted from host's bedroom for steamy reading.

* Offer buck-a-pop peeks at porno mags for under-age guests.

* Using floss and nail scissors, fashion fabulous party dress from see-through shower curtain.

* Drag handsome stranger in with you and just see what happens once the door is locked.

* Lock door, stand in front of mirror, and practice "my ex just walked in but I don't care" look or "I'm not trashed" face or both.

* Roll a joint with tampon wrapper paper.

You know it's time to throw a party when you get a refund check from the IRS.

How to Add Bad to . . . the Holidays!

At Thanksgiving, play *Problem Child!*

Troubled Kleptomaniac Kid: Before the meal is served, take time out to steal small valuables from the host, hostess, and other guests, then stash them in the stuffing, mashed spuds, sweet potatoes, and pumpkin pie. Guests will love to discover these surprises as they make their way through their favorite meal of the year.

Overstimulated ADD Brat: Once the turkey has been carved and the stuffing removed, grab the Thanksgiving bird, pull it onto your head like a helmet, and run around the table with your thumbs jammed in your armpits, flapping your arms and gobbling at the top of your lungs.

Angry Politically Correct Child: Just as everyone is sitting down to enjoy their feast, tap your wine glass with a fork, stand up, and read a one-page speech about the oppression in the United States and why we should all boycott this bogus holiday.

Geeky, Socially Awkward Brainiac: After several large mugs of mulled wine, retreat to the bedroom, don a pilgrim costume, and insist that everyone follow you to the backyard to reenact the age-old tradition of burying three kernels of corn and a dead fish. Be prepared to deliver a brief lecture on the history of the first Thanksgiving.

Bitter Rage-Against-the-Machine Kid: An hour before dinner, remove the fuse to the kitchen from the fuse box and hide it. As a back up, sever the cable wire just before the big football game.

At Christmas, play *Family Secret Santa!*

Most families don't talk enough about the things that really matter—personal feelings, personal needs, or personal sexual preferences. When you play Family Secret Santa, you not only get to open the lines of communication, you get to open gifts! Why repress your family's dirty little secrets when you can wrap them up and put them under the tree?

What you need:
* access to family members' personal belongings
* gift boxes
* wrapping paper
* family secrets

What you do:
Raid family members' bedrooms, suitcases, and closets for that special something that nobody likes to talk about.
   Wrap item in festive holiday paper and place under tree with appropriate name tag. Some suggestions:

* Mom's well-worn vibrator in a gift box with a lovely bow for Dad
* Dad's dirty-magazine collection wrapped up special for Mom
* your sister's junior high yearbook for her new boyfriend
* a framed printout of your brother's personal ad on ComingOut.com for Mom and Dad

glasses to the street below because you love the sound of shattering glass.

* calligraphy transcripts of your therapy sessions for your parents
* a sturdy mobile for Uncle Bob made out of his wife's empty prescription pill bottles
* Dad's empty bourbon bottles filled with flowers for Grandma

More Creative Ways to Add Bad
* Remove and hide all batteries from those noisy, annoying children's toys.
* Unscrew one lightbulb on the tree.
* Don't just sit on Santa's lap, give him a lap dance.
* Secretly mix up the gift cards on all the presents under the tree.
* Give decorated tampon ornaments to all your relatives.

At Hanukkah, play *Spin the Dreidel*
Heat things up for the younger relatives.
* Explain that Spin the Dreidel is played just like Spin the Bottle.
* Grab a tennis racket, play it like an air guitar, and sing at the top of your lungs Van Halen's "Panama," substituting "Hanukkah!"
* Replace the candles in the menorah with sparklers.

You know it's time to throw a party when you've planned your entire wedding,

At Halloween, play *Perverted Private Fantasy!*

Try one of these on for size or live out one of your own!

Florence Naughty-gale *Florence Nightingale in fishnets and a push-up bra*

Eve *Nude body stocking with one fig leaf and two long waves of hair strategically secured*

Dominatrix *Black leather bustier with chains, whips, and boots, baby*

Catholic School Girl *Knee socks, plaid mini skirt rolled up super-short, pigtails, and no undies*

Sexy Professor *Think Van Halen's "Hot for Teacher"*

Lady Cop *Frisk-happy, of course!*

Nancy Drool *A festive frock and a magnifying glass so you can search everywhere for sexy clues*

Wonder Woman *Tight tights, tight leotard, tight red boots, and tight lasso for every hottie you lay eyes on*

Naughty Nun with a bad habit *Fishnets, army boots, tattoos, and garter belt*

named your first three children, and you haven't been on a date in six months.

Making an Exit

Sadly, what you say as you walk away from a conversational cluster is often the only thing anyone remembers. So take the time to plan a personal exit strategy and make sure it packs a memorable punch. Whether you're exiting a dull conversation, an argument you're definitely losing, or bailing on the party altogether, these lines can be your lifesavers!

Casual Conversation Killers

* "I have to check on my kids sleeping in the car. Don't move, I'll be right back."
* "What time is it? Do you have a cell phone? I need to call my parole officer."
* "I'd love to take you home but I probably shouldn't." Lean in and whisper, "I'm in the Witches Protection Program."
* "I haven't had this much fun since (loud snort-laugh) I went to Water World with my co-workers last summer!"
* "I've got a riddle. By the time you get this, I'll be gone."
* "I'd rather have a frontal lobotomy than your body in front of me. Adios."
* "You're it!" (Tag the person and run off.)
* "I really want to get to know you better tonight but this period is a real gusher. Call me in a week?"
* "If you lived here, you'd be home alone by now."

Auto-Argument Enders

* Throw a glass into the fireplace and storm off. (The key is not to say a word!)

You know it's time to leave a party when your lover says he wants to make sweet

Flirting

Ms. Baddy Manners says . . .

* When shopping for a great pair of buns, always try before you buy! As you browse your way through the party, gently caress buns as you would a cantaloupe, checking for shape, texture, firmness, and soft spots.

* Party flirting is like fly fishing: Always employ a gentle catch-and-release policy.

* Always keep your napkin in your lap at a dinner party. Then, if the conversation drags, you can easily entertain yourself.

* Should your napkin fall from your lap, be sure to pick it up promptly and take the opportunity to look under the table for any lap action.

* When moving through a crowded party, kindly signal to other guests your intentions by gently squeezing elbows, buns, or other body parts.

* When flirting in front of a large group, diffuse your nervous excitement by picturing everyone in the room in your underwear.

* Party flirting is like shoe shopping. Try on as many different styles as possible to ensure a snug yet comfortable fit. When you find one you're wild about, charge it!

love to you all night long. You know it's time to throw a party when you've

* Shout, "How dare you!" and slap the arguer across the face.

* Throw a drink in his or her face and firmly state, "You need to cool off!"

* Scream, "I'm telling!" and run out the door.

* Break into hysterical sobs.

* Faint, soap-opera style, into the arms of a handsome stranger.

* Clear the dining room table with one arm and calmly say, "I'm only warning you once."

* Point at the offender and shout, "You! You! You!" until everyone in the room joins in.

Exceptional Party Exit Lines

* "I came for the waterbed. I was misinformed."
* "You won't have Tricia Nixon to kick around anymore!"
* "Would you hold my drink, I see someone I've got to make out with."
* "Please excuse me, the hostess just commissioned me to make a scene."
* "Gotta run. I've got an early flight for a week of Ab Fab Rehab."
* "I'll be right back."
* "There's no place like home. There's no place like home." (Click your heels together and be off!)
* "Hi-ho Silver, away!"
* "Talk to the hand cuz the face don't understand."

re-read—twice—every love letter you've ever received. You know it's time to leave

* Stick arms out at your side like airplane wings and sing, "Off I go, into the wild blue yonder!" as you skip out the door.

* "I came, I saw, I conquered, not in that order, of course."

* Call the host's phone number from your cell phone in the bathroom, put on a fake voice, and say, "Would you please tell (your name) her driver is here?"

* "Bon voyage. I've got places to see and people to do!"

Ms. Baddy Manners says . . . If you find a cute warm someone sleeping under the pile of coats in the guest bedroom, check for signs of life by gently spooning and providing a little mouth-to-mouth resuscitation.

a party when everyone but you has clustered into small groups. You know it's time

Epilogue: The After-Party

It happens to the best of us—the morning after. It's that unexpected, unwanted, unpleasant gift-with-purchase that often accompanies a great party. But why fight it, when you can delight in it? Whether your party afterlife consists of proud memories or loud, throbbing pain (or both), celebrate it! Throw another party, reenact your baddest party favors, work your bad girl image at the office, and make a new list of things to celebrate. Remember: the Party Life is precious and so are you!

Hangover Glossary
Know your symptoms and how to deal.

The Over Easy
You drank a lot last night, but for some strange reason you're feeling no pain. You quickly write down the magi-

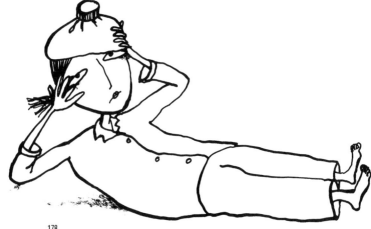

to throw a party when the last time you wore a little black dress was to your

cal equation of food, water, and painkillers you consumed just before bed.

The Layover

Doesn't hit you for a few hours. You wake up feeling better than ever—healthy, alert, funny, smart. You may even mutter the fateful words, "I'm not even hungover!" What you don't know is that you're still drunk. Your hangover should hit in approximately three to four hours. And when it hits, it hits hard.

The Rollover

When you feel so close to death that all you can do is roll over and play dead. Stop hitting snooze, unplug your alarm clock, and sleep. You're lucky you can.

The Over-and-Out

You wake up feeling like hell but decide the best thing to do is get up, get some food, and get on with things. However, once you are up and about you realize that you have made a very big mistake. You should cancel your order, excuse yourself immediately, and return to bed to sleep it off before something ugly happens.

uncle's wake. You know it's time to leave a party when the jug wine comes out. You

The Over Haul

You wake up full of regret. You swore you wouldn't do this again. You hate yourself, and your head and stomach are churning. To alleviate the guilt, you leap from bed, throw on your spandex, and run five miles. You come home, scrub the kitchen floors, clean out your closet, and rearrange the living room furniture (also known as the Over Kill, the Over Drive, and the Over Compensation).

The Tip Over

On top of a nasty headache, queasy stomach, and dry mouth, you're also incredibly uncoordinated and find yourself bumping into everything—when you're able to stand up at all.

The Game Over

You vow never ever to drink again—and then you tell all your friends of your big decision, hoping they'll remind you of it next weekend.

The Makeover

When you see yourself in the mirror and realize the damage done, you blindly grope for foundation, bronzer, eyeliner, mascara, and lipstick. The only way you'll feel any better is if you look better. Even if you're just going back to bed.

know it's time to throw a party when the dirtiest thing you've done in ages is

The Think Over

You lie in bed feeling horrible, trying to count how many drinks you actually consumed, and thinking about embarrassing things you said, outrageous things you did, and the fact that you'll never behave like that ever again (also known as the Go Over, the Over View, and the Overhead Projector).

The Pop Over

You pop as many pills as you can get your hands on. Vitamin B, Vitamin C, aspirin, Advil, Tums, Alka-Seltzer (also known as the Over Dosage and the Over the Counter).

The Do Over

You go out and do it all again. After all, one of the surest hangover cures is another drink (although you're just setting yourself up for a Layover).

The Pass Over

You are lying in bed feeling like crap, trying to go back to sleep, when you feel a warm body part brush against the small of your back. You are not alone! You make an under-the-covers pass, hoping a little action will distract you from your pain. But then realize you're feeling so hungover that you'll have to pass.

The Get Over

You spend your day rationalizing your behavior, talking on the phone only to friends who will rationalize your behavior, and ultimately convincing yourself that your behavior wasn't that bad until, miraculously, you get over it.

change a diaper. You know it's time to leave a party when you forget the story

How to Make a Scary Mary

This kick-ass Bloody Mary is sure to cure what ails you.

What you need:
2 shots of Absolut Peppar vodka
3 drops of Tabasco sauce
1 teaspoon Worcestershire sauce
3 ounces of tomato or V8 juice
fresh ground pepper and sea salt
fresh lemon juice
Cajun spices
2 aspirin
2 Alka-Seltzer
fresh celery stalk
lime wedge

What you do:
Crush the Alka-Seltzer and aspirin into a fine powder and mix with Cajun spices.

Wet the rim of a large glass with lemon juice, then dust with Cajun painkilling spices.

Mix all ingredients and shake with ice, then strain into the glass over ice cubes. Add celery, a squeeze of lemon, and the wedge of lime. Drink with attitude.

Ms. Baddy Manners says . . . When nursing a nasty hangover, mix a Scary Mary with plenty of ice, pour it into an ice pack bag, then close the screw top tightly. Press against forehead and the back of the neck, then open and sip as needed.

The Bad Hangover Party

Your mouth tastes like the Sahara, your brain feels three sizes too big for your skull, the room is spinning, it's way too bright, and who's that lump in bed next to you? Oh wait! This isn't your bed. Wherever you find yourself, whenever you come to, now is the right time to get on the horn, round up the troops, and bring them together for an all-day Bad Hangover Party.

Ms. Baddy Manners says . . . If you can't sneak out the back door (or the dog door) before dawn, then be sure to whip up a fabulous hangover-helper breakfast for you, the host, and any other party stragglers!

Guest List: Your bad girl accomplices from the night before. (You weren't the only one dancing on the bar, were you?)

Invitations: Hit your speed dial and assign each guest to make a quick pit stop on her way over to pick up some of the following hangover helpers from your menu, shopping list, and prep work lists. (You're simply too weak to do a thing!)

Attire:
* Smudged makeup
* Smoky day-after hair tied back far from sensitive nose in a messy mess
* Walk of Shame survivors must remain in sexy, now-rumpled outfit from the previous night.
* Pajamas are allowed only for those who actually slept in them.

you are telling in the middle of telling it. You know it's time to throw a party when

Prep Work: Rent movies that don't take much concentration but provide nice, lighthearted entertainment. A comedy like *Clueless* or *When Harry Met Sally* works, or something soothing from your past like *The Breakfast Club, About Last Night,* or *Sixteen Candles.* Tear-jerkers like *Terms of Endearment* are also recommended, as crying will release toxins and make you feel better. Another tactic is to rent a movie that will put the room to sleep (nothing heals like a good nap). Try *Eyes Wide Shut* or any Kubrick film.

Shopping List: Each person is assigned a different category from the Hangover Food Pyramid.

* economy-sized bottle of Extra-Strength Tylenol and/or Advil
* economy-sized bottle of Tums
* anti-oxidant vitamins (If you believe B-6 works, it will!)
* vodka, tomato juice, lemons, Worcestershire sauce
* eggs, bacon, and potatoes for your famous greasy home-fried Hangover Helper

you care what Howard Stern thinks. You know it's time to leave a party when

* Coca-Cola, Alka-Seltzer
* saltines, Pringles, Ruffles, Doritos, Fritos, Cheetos
* Ho-Ho's, Ding Dongs, Ring Dings, Chips Ahoy

Decor: Remove all bedding—pillows, down comforters, quilts—and place on living room sofas, chairs, and floor (if carpeted). Accent with sleeping bags.

Pull down shades, dim lights. Light soothing aroma-therapy candles.

Mood Music: Enya, rain forest sounds

Special Touch: Ice packs and/or chilled gel eye-masks

Party Games: *Pop-Up Memories!* Throughout the day, nearly forgotten memories from the previous night's activities will randomly pop into guests' throbbing heads. As they do, guests must scream "Pop-up memory!" and reveal their hilarious and/or horrifying tales.

Live Reenactments. When a pop-up memory occurs that involves a fellow guest doing something bad (i.e., dancing on bar, macking on bartender, telling a tall tale), the guest must reenact the scene for all to see. Tape or video record to capture those hilarious horror stories.

Walk of Shame Confessions. Anyone who performed a Walk of Shame the night before must stand up and confess with a full, blow-by-blow account of all the dirt.

Party Favors: Each guest receives a fistfull of antacids, a jumbo bottle of water, and AA literature.

you've said goodbye to everyone so many times that they've stopped responding.

Cozy Places to Crash

Sometimes a party is so great you just don't want to leave—and then you can't because (whoops!) your ride already did. Other times you know you should leave but you can't find the door through your booze goggles. Not to worry! Why go home at all when there are so many cozy places at a party to curl up and spend the night? Try these mini crash pads and see how comfortable you can be!

* your host's closet floor

* the bathtub

* the crawl space behind a sofa

* a large dog bed

* tree fort

* dirty laundry basket

* inside a long window seat

* under the dining room table (or any table with a long tablecloth)

* beanbag chair in the kid's room (Shhhh. Don't wake the kid.)

* on a sturdy hedge

* inside that sea kayak in the garage

* a hammock

keeping your bad girl
image alive and kickin'

Like all of the finer things in the Party Life, maintaining your bad girl image requires training, practice, and a genuine commitment to your craft. When you make the extra effort, it shows in your performance—and people notice and want to be near you. Try a few of these sure-fire techniques for building your image.

* Start your day by gargling with a large mouthful of bourbon or Scotch.

* When riding the bus or subway to work, mingle, network, and meet new people.

* Show up at work drinking your morning coffee out of a martini glass.

* Fashion a creative scarf out of last night's hot pink party streamers.

* Drink your eight glasses of water a day, straight up with a twist.

* Circulate through your staff meeting with a tray of tasty hors d'oeuvres.

* In a voice loud enough for everyone in your office to hear you, call an expensive catering company and ask if they can cater a spontaneous formal event tonight for about 50 people.

* Add face and body glitter to your normal daily makeup routine.

You know it's time to throw a party when you offer to baby-sit on the weekend.

* Show up at work wearing dark sunglasses and popping Altoids out of an Extra-Strength Tylenol bottle. When asked if you're all right, just mutter something about last night, then chuckle.

* Forfeit boring gym routines for a solo dance party in your own living room—be sure to crank the music until your neighbors pound on the wall.

* Wear the men's XL cologne-scented sweater you found behind the sofa all week long.

* Instead of washing your face, preserve your darkly smudged kohl eyeliner and mascara all week long.

* Show up at work in last night's rumpled party clothes—fishnets, leather mini, suede go-go boots—and smile naughtily when colleagues shoot you suspicious looks.

* Fill in your daily planner with parties every night of the week and leave it open on your desk at the office.

* When bored at work, create fabulous party evites for faux parties at nonexistent locations and send them to everyone you know.

* Give yourself a neck hickey.

You know it's time to leave a party when your beer goggles start to work. You

How to Give Yourself a Neck Hickey

What you need:
* a snorkel
* no shame

What you do:
Select a realistic target spot on your neck.

Place the mouthpiece of the snorkel firmly against the skin of your neck (the mouthpiece on skin ensures a natural and believable hickey shape).

Place the other end of the snorkel in your mouth.

Suck like you mean it for about 30 seconds. Repeat if necessary.

If you can't locate a snorkel, feel free to substitute a Dust Buster or other small hand vacuum—and be sure to use the most lip-like attachment. Do not use a full-size, full-power vacuum unless you want people to think that you've been getting it on with a vacuum.

More Excuses to Throw a Party

Looking for more occasions to celebrate? Here are some popular bad girl dates you shouldn't miss:

Blame Someone Else Day — January 13

Man Watchers' Week — January 8–14

Answer Your Cat's Question Day — January 22

Panic Day — March 9

National Girl Scout Day — March 12

National Dance Like a Chicken Day — May 13

True Confessions Day — March 15

Don't Go to Work Unless It's Fun Day — April 3

Lost Sock Memorial Day — May 9

Let It Go Day — June 23

Bra Burning Day — June 27

National Nude Day — July 14

Crank Call Day — July 17

National Failures Day — August 5

Get Out of Town Day — September 21

Mischief Night (England) — November 4

National Doughnut Day — November 5

Wear a Plunger on Your Head Day — December 18

The Strut of Pride

When heading home in the light of day after a wild night of celebrating, don't sneak or cower—feel your bad girl power! The Walk of Shame is for good girls. A genuine bad girl does the Strut of Pride on the morning after. Wherever you end up the next day, know that you've lived, celebrated your life, and had a good ole bad girl time. With the right attitude, you can turn the Strut of Pride into your own private party.

Perfecting the Strut of Pride

* Stride out and strut like you mean it.
* Wink and smirk at nosy busybodies.
* Wave and smile at anyone you know.
* Notice the color of the sky.
* Go directly to church and sit in the front row.
* Play with pets and young children.
* Dance to the music in your head.
* Laugh at yourself.
* Tell your stories to strangers on the bus.
* Make a mental list of all the new things to celebrate.
* Plan your next party!

Ms. Baddy Manners says . . . Pack a small Bible in your evening bag before heading out to a party. When doing the Strut of Pride, pull it out and hold it in plain view. If anyone asks where you worship, smile and proudly say, "The church of Badder Day Saints!"

know it's time to throw a party when you ask the mailman if he'd like to come in

About the Author

Cameron Tuttle is the author of the best-selling *The Bad Girl's Guide to the Open Road* and *The Bad Girl's Guide to Getting What You Want,* as well as *The Paranoid's Pocket Guide,* all from Chronicle Books. She lives *la vida* Bad Girl in San Francisco.

About the Illustrator

Susannah Bettag is the ultimate bad girl. Her brilliant illustrations have appeared in *The Bad Girl's Guide to the Open Road* and *The Bad Girl's Guide to Getting What You Want* as well as in numerous magazines. When she's not painting or snowboarding, she's riding her motorcycle very, very fast. She lives the party life in San Francisco.

Go to badgirlswirl.com to reach the author and illustrator and to mix it up with other bad girls.

for a drink. You know it's time to leave a party when you're late for another party!